Insider's Guide to **Horseracing**

CONTENTS

In loving memory of H. Dean Montgomery, thoroughbred trainer, and Frank Y. Whiteley Jr., a horseman with no equal

CONTENTS

INTRODUCTION

The *Insider's Guide to Horseracing* was written to help the average race goer to better understand the sport of horseracing from the standpoint of a professional horse person. This book is different from any other in the literature of horseracing. It is neither about the legendary horses nor their human counterparts who decorate the annals of history. This book will not reveal any scheme or magic formula to pick winners at the races. It is the intention of this book to present a general outlook in the hope that one small piece of information might assist the average race goer in some small way. Many racing fans simply place a wager on a horse with little or no planning. Their wager may be influenced by the horse's name, the color of the horse's coat, or the color of the jockey's silks. The *Insider's Guide to Horseracing* will allow the reader to make an intelligent wager and have a more enjoyable time at the racetrack. The racetrack should be approached as a day's outing, like going to the beach. Even if you didn't get to go in the water, it was good to get away, and it was fun.

Too many racing fans know little or nothing about horseracing other than to recognize it as a fascinating sport. People, as a general rule, know very little about the development and training of a racehorse. Horseracing is a big business.

In the spring of 2004, a horse by the name of Smarty Jones took the American public on a joyous ride in his quest to win the Triple Crown of racing. A small horse by breed standards from a small track (Philadelphia Park) with a trainer, owner, and jockey that had never competed in any classic race,

1

Smarty Jones was undefeated going into the Kentucky Derby at Churchill Downs, the first jewel of the Triple Crown. When it was over, he had defeated some of the best 3-year-old colts in the country. Still undefeated, he was set for the Preakness Stakes, the second jewel of the Triple Crown, held at Pimlico Racetrack in Baltimore, Maryland. He annihilated his opponents by winning by almost 12 lengths. All that remained was the final jewel of the Triple Crown: the Belmont Stakes—a mile and a half, held at Belmont Park, New York.

Not since the famed Seattle Slew—Triple Crown winner in 1977—had a horse had the opportunity to win the Triple Crown undefeated. Only 11 horses in the history of racing have won the Triple Crown. In the eyes of America, Smarty Jones was the "little horse that could."

On June 5, 2004, he suffered his first defeat in the Belmont Stakes by finishing second to the winner Birdstone. Smarty Jones not only had to overcome his rivals in each race but he also had to overcome those ever-present obstacles found in every racehorse's career, including physical infirmities, poor track conditions, unfavorable post position, unfavorable distance, unfavorable pace, poor start, high weight impost, faulty equipment, and poor jockey decision. These variable factors are always present throughout the racing career of every racehorse. Each year breeders, owners, and trainers hope to produce a champion racehorse, but champions like Smarty Jones are few and far between. Well-bred yearlings sell for millions of dollars and rarely win back their purchase price on the racetrack.

I wanted to produce a book that would not only be of educational value but would prove to be profitable to the hordes of Americans who annually spend millions of their hard-earned dollars at the turnstiles and mutual windows of the many racetracks found in this country. I do hope this book fulfills the reader's expectations in understanding one of the greatest sports known to mankind. Horseracing is not only a sport but it is also a recreation and a business that has proven its popularity. It is here to stay.

Good Luck!

HISTORY OF
THOROUGHBRED RACING

In ancient Egypt, the use of horse-drawn chariots prevailed, but it was the ancient Greeks who developed chariot racing as the world's first wagering sport. At the first Olympic Games, chariot racing took center stage. By 680 B.C., the sport became a regular part of the games and started to attract the interest of royalty.

When Caesar came to the British Isles in 50 B.C., British horses were hardy and small in size. Size and weight became increasingly important in warfare as chariots were abandoned and the knight in heavy armor became the ideal fighting unit.

The development of the light horse became inevitable as warfare became modernized and the armored knight became outdated. The light horses found in England were usually small in size (under 14 hands), which was too small to fulfill the requirements of the cavalry. What was needed was a type of horse that was as tall as the heavier horses but lighter in weight—a horse that could combine speed and stamina. A horse with these characteristics would satisfy both military and racing requirements.

As early as the reign of Henry VIII in the early 1500s there was a royal stud. Henry VIII was an enormous racing enthusiast and is considered to be one of the founders of modern horseracing. During his reign, there was racing at Chester and later at Doncaster, where a racetrack was built in 1595.

Horseracing became known as the Sport of Kings under the zealous horseman Charles II. Charles himself rode in races. Flat racing actually began during his reign. Prior to that time, most racing had been an informal variation of steeplechase racing (jumping hurdles during a race). Racing in the seventeenth and eighteenth centuries was quite different from what it is today. Usually races were matches between 2 horses (sometimes 3 or 4). It should be understood that racehorses during that time period had to travel to race meets on their own legs, since horse vans did not appear until 1816. There were no grandstands, so spectators had to view the races from horseback or in carriages. Prizes consisted of private stakes, though the government established a series of King's Plates to encourage improvement of the horse. This was achieved in England through 3 imported stallions: the Darley Arabian, the Godolphin Arabian, and the Byerly Turk. These 3 stallions would become the foundation sires of the breed that would be known as the Thoroughbred. Of these 3 foundation sires, the Darley Arabian was the only purebred Arabian. The Godolphin Arabian and Byerly Turk were each a cross between the Turcoman and Arabian breeds.

The Byerly Turk was imported to England in 1689 and was bred to predominately small English mares. His great-great-grandson Herod founded one of the 3 foundation lines of the Thoroughbred. The Darley Arabian was brought to England in 1706. His great-great-grandson Eclipse founded another foundation line of the breed. Eclipse was a superior racehorse; he was unbeaten in 26 starts and was the first great Thoroughbred to emerge after the Thoroughbred became recognized as a breed. The Godolphin Arabian was the last of the 3 to be imported to England in the 1720s. His grandson Matchem was also instrumental in establishing a dominant male line within the breed.

Although horseracing had become an established sport, neither racing nor breeding became a matter of public record

Grand Sweepstakes at Pimlico, October 24, 1877, featuring Parole, Ten Broeck, and Tom Ochiltree. Congress, for the first time in its history, adjourned for this race. (From *Blooded Horses of Colonial Days* by Frances Culver)

until well into the eighteenth century when James Weatherby published *An Introduction to a General Stud Book.* Thus it can be said that it was in the beginning reign of George I that the Thoroughbred finally became recognized as a separate breed of horse. The name Thoroughbred, however, did not come into general use until about 1808.

Those Englishmen who came to America in the early 1600s brought with them their enthusiasm for horseracing. Racing was conducted on the streets of the early settlements. The streets were short, which led to a type of horseracing that became typical of early America—short dashes, with an emphasis on speed and rapid starts. Of course, this sprint racing was not like the horseracing found in England.

The first racecourse in the new colonies was probably the Newmarket Course, built on the Hempstead plains on Long Island in 1665 by New York Governor Nicolls. It was established as the first area in America to have organized racing. In 1730, the Darley Arabian's son named Bulle Rock became the first recognized Thoroughbred to be imported from England to the colony of Virginia in America. In 1798, the Thoroughbred stallion Diomed was shipped to America.

Saratoga race track, Saratoga Springs, New York, about 1910. (LC-D4-39407)

Diomed was an English castoff who had a major role in establishing the Thoroughbred in America. He was the winner of the first running of the Epsom Derby in 1780. Among Diomed's offspring was the first American champion, Sir Archy.

Lexington, who led American sires 16 times, beginning in 1861, was descended from Diomed through sires Sir Archy, Timoleon, and Boston.

After the American Revolution, Americans naturally turned away from traditional English customs. In 1777, the North Carolina Assembly introduced a law to halt all horseracing. In 1792, the Virginia Assembly limited wagering to no more than $7.00 on any horse race. Pennsylvania, New Jersey, and New York also introduced legislative measures to hinder the progress of horseracing. However, in the great westward expansion to the Pacific Ocean, the horse continued to play an important role, and the racing and breeding of horses began to gain momentum throughout the new land.

Kentucky, Alabama, Tennessee, Georgia, and Ohio emerged as major horse-breeding centers, and racetracks appeared in Chicago, St. Louis, Louisiana, and California.

Shortly after the Revolution, Richmond, Virginia, became the horseracing capital of America with 3 formal racetracks: Tree Hill, Fairfield, and Broad Rock. In Massachusetts, a racetrack was opened in the city of Medford in 1811.

After the damages of the War of 1812 were repaired, the city of Baltimore boasted of 2 racetracks within walking distance of the city. The Union Course, located on Long Island in New York, was opened in 1821 and soon became the model of all racetracks for the future. In 1840, Chicago built 2 racetracks. One was 4 miles in circumference, and the second was a 1-mile track within the infield of the first. The first formal racetrack to open in California was Pioneer Course in 1851. It was located in San Francisco and operated under the rules of the Union Jockey Club of New York. Saratoga Racecourse opened on August 2, 1864, and is the oldest existing racetrack in America. It is located in beautiful Saratoga Springs, New York. It has become known as the graveyard of champions, as it was the site for many great upsets in Thoroughbred racing. Examples include Man O' War's only defeat to a horse called Upset in 1919, Triple Crown winner Gallant Fox's 1930 loss to Jim Dandy, and the great Secretariat's defeat to a horse called Onion in 1973. Today, Saratoga Racecourse is considered to be the home of the finest Thoroughbred racing in the world with horses coming from different countries to compete each August. Pimlico Racecourse had its inaugural meet in 1870. Located in Baltimore, Maryland, it is the site for the second jewel of the Triple Crown: the Preakness Stakes. This prestigious event was first run in 1873 and was named after the colt Preakness who was a son of the famous sire Lexington. The Louisville Jockey Club held its inaugural race meet in 1875 that later became known as Churchill Downs. The feature race that year was contested at a distance of 1 1/2 miles for 3 year olds with the winner's share of the purse at $2,850.00. The race has become known as the Kentucky Derby, the most famous horse race in America.

Throughout the nineteenth century, horseracing became organized and progressed with shorter races and higher purses. In 1894, through the efforts of James R. Keene, the American Jockey Club took over complete control of horseracing. The Jockey Club purchased the American Stud Book in 1896. It wrote the rules, granted racing dates, issued licenses to trainers and jockeys, and appointed racing officials. As Thoroughbred racing broadened over the years, throughout the nation the authority of the Jockey Club declined. Individual state racing commissions were formed as parimutuel wagering was approved. Duties and functions formerly assumed by the Jockey Club were absorbed by racing commissions. However, the Jockey Club still retained the task of maintaining the official Stud Book. A horse cannot be considered a Thoroughbred unless it is so registered by the Jockey Club. Horseracing in America has gained in popularity over the years due to many underlying factors, including the creation of the *American Stud Book*, the American Jockey Club, and the introduction of pari-mutuel wagering. However, the most important factor for the success of Thoroughbred racing in America is the charm and lure of the horses themselves. Outstanding individuals such as Man O' War, Whirlaway, Seabiscuit, Citation, Secretariat, Seattle Slew, Affirmed, and countless others have become household words and national heroes.

In the year 2001, America embraced the book entitled *Seabiscuit: An American Legend* by Laura Hillenbrand. Through this best-selling book and successful motion picture in 2003, the legendary Seabiscuit launched horseracing into the limelight of sports entertainment just as he had done dur-

Seabiscuit (second from left) making his spectacular move in the final turn of the 1940 Santa Anita Handicap, a race that sealed the thoroughbred's legendary status. (From *Seabiscuit: Saga of a Great Champion* by B. K. Beckwith)

ing the Depression years of the 1930s. Seabiscuit, the former has-been of horseracing, defeated Triple Crown winner War Admiral in a match race at Pimlico Racecourse on November 1, 1938. He won by 4 lengths and set a new track record for the 1 3/16-mile distance. At 7 years of age, Seabiscuit retired in 1940 as the world's leading money winner with a total of $437,730.00.

Seabiscuit's "rags-to-riches" story generated an enormous interest in the sport of horseracing. Many new fans are learning that there is almost nothing more satisfying than to cheer a horse on to victory, while the anticipation of the next great horse's appearance, perhaps as winner of the elusive Triple Crown, provides additional excitement unrivaled in the sports world.

2

BEHIND THE SCENES

Despite the obvious differences in customs and language, horse races possess a similarity that exists throughout the world. A mixture of spectators made up of a true cross section of society fill the grandstands, no matter where the racetrack is located. As you enter a racetrack, you immediately experience the excitement in the air. Vendors are hawking programs and newspapers, food, and souvenirs. Patrons are scurrying about everywhere in order to get their wagers in before post time. As you walk through the grandstand and you cast your eyes on the vast oval of the racetrack for the first time, it takes your breath away. I can only compare the feeling to what a child at a baseball stadium for the first time feels when he or she emerges from a dark tunnel leading to the first view of the enormous playing field. It's a sight and feeling that you will never forget for as long as you live. All your senses are heightened with the brilliant colors of the racetrack reflected through the green turf, the flowers and trees, the jockey's silks, and the horses themselves. The announcer voices the words "They're off," and the roar of the crowd as the horses race down the long homestretch is deafening. When you analyze the sport of horseracing, it is the horse that is the main attraction. The Thoroughbred with its grace, courage, and speed is considered to be the foundation of the sport. Once exposed to the sport of horseracing, you stay with it the rest of your life, and it becomes difficult to abandon.

The average race goer, though, has no conception of what goes on behind the scenes at a racetrack. They are oblivious of the fact that there are scores of professionals behind each race. This behind-the-scenes world at any major racetrack can be divided into 2 separate factions: the FRONTSIDE and the BACKSIDE.

The frontside consists of those officials responsible for conducting a race meet. The backside consists of those individuals that are directly involved with the daily care and training of the horses stabled at the racetrack. There is no sport that is as stringently supervised and policed as is horseracing. Now and then there may be an isolated incident of criminal activity, but for the most part, the sport of horseracing is honest.

Frontside

There are several racing officials employed at each racetrack who are responsible for conducting racing each day. Officials are usually appointed or approved by the state racing commission. Racing officials at any racetrack include the following positions:

RACING STEWARDS

RACING SECRETARY

CLERK OF SCALES

PATROL JUDGES

TIMER

PADDOCK JUDGE

STARTER

STATE VETERINARIAN

IDENTIFIER

PLACING JUDGE

Naturally, the lower level of the racing organization consists of maintenance and clerical staff.

RACING STEWARDS: The stewards are by far the most important officials at any racetrack. They have very broad duties and enormous power. There are usually 3 stewards at a race meet; one usually represents the association conducting the meeting, another represents the Jockey Club, and a third represents the state racing commission. The stewards are responsible for enforcing the rules of racing. They will conduct hearings and impose penalties when required.

RACING SECRETARY: Racing secretaries are responsible for designing the daily racing program from the horses available for racing at the track. They must also design a permanent stakes schedule for a particular race meeting as well as assign weights for handicap races. Periodically the racing secretary develops a daily program through the use of a condition book. The condition book is used by the owners and trainers to determine the eligibility of each horse in their stable for a particular race. The condition book details each race for approximately a 12-day period. The upcoming races are listed according to age, distance, turf, claiming price, sex, weight assignment, and amount of purse and eligibility requirements.

CLERK OF SCALES: The duty of the clerk of scales is to keep a record of the jockey's weights. All riders must report to the clerk of scales and state what their weight will be for each of the races in which they are assigned a mount. They must also report the equipment they will be utilizing. The clerk of scales is required to weigh each jockey before and after each race before a race can be declared official.

PATROL JUDGE: The patrol judge is required to observe the running of a race from beginning to end and report directly to the stewards any infractions on the part of the jockeys and horses during the race. Their observations are supplemented by cameras recording each race from various strategic positions throughout the racetrack. In the event of an infraction, the stewards will determine the severity of punishment and the official results of a particular race based on the reports of the patrol judges and their review of the recorded tape of a race in question.

TIMER: The role of the official timer is to time each race from beginning to end. It is a duty that supplements an electric timing device. Electric timers are considered more accurate than their human counterparts. Most major racetracks utilize an electric timing device to record the official time of a race. There are some racetracks that require the official timer to time morning workouts of the horses in training.

PADDOCK JUDGE: Before each race, the paddock judge is responsible for seeing that each horse is racing in the proper equipment. Racing equipment includes blinkers, breastplate, tongue-tie, bandages, etc. The paddock judge will announce "riders up" so that the post parade of entries can begin their trek to the starting gate.

STARTER: The starter is responsible for a fair and safe start for every race. The starter supervises the loading of each horse by the assistant starters into the starting gate. When all the horses are standing quiet in the starting gate and all the jockeys are ready, the starter will then release the field from the gate, and the race will officially begin.

STATE VETERINARIAN: The state veterinarian is required to observe every horse before the running of a race in the saddling paddock. The veterinarian is also required to observe all the horses as they are being loaded into the starting gate. If any physical abnormalities are noted in the paddock or starting gate, the state veterinarian has the power to scratch a horse from a race. Should a horse unseat its rider and get loose prior to the start of a race, it is the duty of the state veterinarian to determine if the horse should be scratched or allowed to run. Finally, the state veterinarian will attend to any horse that may have been injured during or after a race.

IDENTIFIER: The identifier is usually employed by the racetrack or racing association. The responsibility of the identifier is to verify the identity of each horse stabled on the racetrack grounds. The identifier personally inspects each horse in each race by referring to the foal certificate and making note of the horse's lip tattoo, body color, scars, and head and leg markings.

PLACING JUDGE: The placing judge is usually stationed above the finish line. He or she is responsible for viewing the finish of each race and declaring the official order of finish. At the end of each race, the official order of finish is posted on the infield tote board of the racetrack. The placing judge is also required to transfer photographs of the finish of each race to the stewards for official rulings.

Backside

The backside of the racetrack consists of those professional horse people that work directly with the horses, including:

TRAINER

GROOM

HOT WALKER

EXERCISE RIDER

FARRIER

TRACK SUPERINTENDENT

OUTRIDER

JOCKEY VALET

TRAINER: The basic duty of trainers is to assess the potential of the horses placed in their care. They must supervise employees who exercise, feed, and provide the general care for the horses. Income for a trainer is based on a daily rate from $25.00 to more than $100.00 per day. In addition to the daily rate, trainers receive a standard 10% of their horse's earnings. The role of the trainer will be discussed in more detail in chapter 9.

GROOM: The groom is responsible for the feeding, watering, and general well-being of the horse. He or she must clean out the stalls each day as well as bathe the horse after a race or workout. The groom must lead the racehorse to and from the saddling paddock before and after a race. One groom is usually responsible for the care of 3 horses in a racing stable.

HOT WALKER: The basic function of the hot walker is to walk a hot racehorse after a race or a workout. The purpose of walking a hot horse is to bring its body temperature back down to normal after it has raced or exercised. Hot walkers may be required to assist in the daily stable chores such as bathing, grazing, feeding, raking, and watering.

EXERCISE RIDER: The exercise rider is responsible for riding the racehorse during morning exercise sessions on the track. The exercise rider is also responsible for getting the racehorse accustomed to the starting gate. Like the hot walker, an exercise rider also assists in performing the daily stable chores.

FARRIER: Farriers, or blacksmiths/horseshoers, are responsible for selecting the types of horseshoes that will best fit the horse and aid the horse in racing. They must fit, shape, and secure the shoes to the horse's hooves. The farrier must routinely examine the feet of the racehorse for any deformities or ailments.

TRACK SUPERINTENDENT: Although track superintendents are part of the frontside administration, their work is confined to the backside. Track superintendents are usually employed by the racetrack or the racing association conducting the race meets. They are responsible for maintaining the condition of the racing strip. Before a race meet actually begins, the track superintendent directs the maintenance crew to remove the sandy cushion in order to inspect the clay base for worn spots and make repairs. The sandy cushion is replaced over the clay base and rolled so that the top layer is smooth and hard. Packing the surface tight with rollers allows the water to run off the surface with little penetration. When racing begins, the maintenance crews water, harrow, and rake the track as well as filter the sandy cushion to remove small stones. On the turf courses, the track superintendent and the maintenance crew must repair worn spots and plant new seed. They must also mow the turf to the proper height. After the morning training session is over, the racing strip is then harrowed and groomed and made ready for the afternoon races. The track is also watered and harrowed before and after each race.

OUTRIDER: Much like the track superintendent, the outrider is employed by the racetrack. During the morning training sessions, outriders are mounted on horses, and they are responsible for the safety of the riders. They enforce the rules that govern the training period in the mornings. They are required to assist a rider in controlling an unruly horse. If a rider is thrown to the ground, the outrider will assist the rider and secure an ambulance if necessary. The outrider will also capture a loose horse and return the horse to the trainer or groom. There are usually 2 outriders on duty during the morning training session. In the afternoon while racing is going on, the outrider will lead the horses in the post parade to the starting gate. Once the horses are loaded in the gate, the outrider is positioned on horseback in front of the gate on the outside rail awaiting the start. If a horse breaks through the gate before the official start, the outrider will capture the racehorse from atop his/her horse and return it to the starting gate. At the end of each race, the outrider is available to any jockeys requiring assistance in pulling up their horses.

JOCKEY VALET: The jockey valets provide a vital service to the jockey by laying out the proper silks for each race along with the jockey's helmet, boots, breeches, safety vest, saddle, girths, and goggles. The valet is required to clean and polish the jockey's boots and saddle on a regular basis. One of the most important duties is to assist the trainer in tacking and untacking the racehorse before and after each race. A valet may provide a service to more than one jockey, depending on the number of riders located at the racetrack. The jockey valet is usually employed by the racetrack management, and in addition to a regular salary, he or she may receive 3% to 5% of the jockey's earnings.

DEVELOPMENT OF THE RACEHORSE

There are various types of horseracing that exist throughout the world. Racing fans can enjoy Standardbred racing in which trotters and pacers race by pulling a sulky (2-wheeled cart) with a driver in control. Quarter Horse racing is contested at short distances from 220 yards to 440 yards. Most Quarter Horse racing is performed on a straightaway from the starting gate to the finish line. Arabian horses race at distances of 2 miles or more. The Arabian breed is known for its endurance and stamina.

Thoroughbred Characteristics

Although there are many different types of racehorses representing various breeds, the Thoroughbred stands alone as the world's supreme racehorse. The Thoroughbred is unique in that not all Thoroughbreds are suited for the rigors of racing. The selection criteria of a Thoroughbred racehorse consist of many different characteristics. The professional horse person should take into consideration the following characteristics.

PEDIGREE: The pedigree, or lineage, of a horse's family is a valuable tool in determining a horse's racing potential and value. Comparing an individual's pedigree with similar pedigrees of successful racehorses serves as a viable indicator of a horse's racing ability. The presence of outstanding individuals in a pedigree does not guarantee that the offspring will inherit favorable genes. These favorable gene combinations may not transfer from parent to offspring.

PERFORMANCE: This is the most important factor to consider when selecting a racehorse. One should review a horse's racing record to determine whether the horse has maintained a high level of performance for several months. The most common factors affecting a horse's performance are track conditions, training, nutrition, age, and sex. In selecting a racehorse, one must consider the number of times a horse has raced, the status of the racetracks where it has raced, and the conditions under which the horse has competed.

CONFORMATION: This aspect of selection refers to the physical makeup and the bodily proportions of the horse. A horse should have a balanced structure free of any conformation faults that may lead to unsoundness. A horse with good conformation will perform well with less chance of infirmities. A Thoroughbred with good conformation will exhibit the following features:

A refined, intelligent head

A long, elegant neck

Long, sloping shoulders

A strong body with depth extending through the girth area

Well-muscled hind quarters

Long, straight limbs with well-defined knees and hocks

Many conformation faults can affect a horse's ability to function in a normal fashion and can lead to serious lameness. The type and degree of unsoundness must be considered before a horse can be used for racing. For example, a wide foot with a thick hoof wall is preferred over a small foot with a thin hoof wall. The foot supports the entire weight of the horse's body, therefore, a large, wide foot is preferred to allow the horse to withstand the stress of racing. Many trainers believe that a horse with a large, wide foot will perform well on a turf course and a muddy surface.

SIZE: The size of a Thoroughbred (or any horse for that matter) is measured in hands. Each hand is equivalent to 4 inches. The height of a horse is measured from the highest point of the withers to the ground (Figure 3-1). An average Thoroughbred will measure between 15 and 17 hands in height. A small racehorse with the will to win can easily defeat a larger horse in a race. A racehorse (large or small) with a long stride will usually have long forearms on the front legs and long gaskins on the hind legs. A stride is a horse's way of going, or the linear distance covered (over 20 feet) after each foot has hit the ground once.

TEMPERAMENT: A quiet disposition is an important quality in a racehorse. Quiet horses are less likely to injure themselves, their handlers, and the horses around them. Most professional horse people agree that temperament is an inheritable trait. It has been determined through research that the mare has more of an influence on the foal's temperament than does the stallion. A quiet, gentle mare is more apt to produce a foal with a good disposition than will a mare that is ill tempered. Temperament is also influenced by a horse's environment. A racehorse is isolated in a stall for up to 22 hours a day with little or no contact with other horses. The horse is a herd animal, and interaction with herd members is essential to their psychological well-being. Placing a racehorse in an isolated environment can create a situation in which some horses develop bad habits such as biting, chewing, kicking, or stall walking.

TRAINING: A horse must have certain mental and physical characteristics that will make it suitable for a specific task. A horse that responds favorably to humans, exhibits interest in its surroundings, and is eager to learn with little or no resistance is more trainable than a horse that possesses stubborn

Height at the withers

3-1. The height of a horse is measured from the highest point of the withers to the ground. An average Thoroughbred will measure between 15 and 17 hands. (Author)

qualities. A good racehorse trainer will observe the horse on a daily basis while in his or her care. It is through this practice that the trainer soon learns of a horse's likes and dislikes. The following are just some of the many likes and dislikes a horse will express to its trainer:

Some racehorses do not like mud hitting them in the face during a race or workout.

There are those racehorses that prefer to run in front of the field, while others prefer to run behind the leaders.

Some racehorses prefer to run over turf as opposed to a dirt surface.

Some horses prefer short sprint races, while others prefer long-distance races.

There are those horses that prefer to exercise in the early morning before dawn.

Some horses do not like to be touched or groomed on certain parts of their body such as the head or rear flanks.

Some horses will eat their grain very rapidly, while others take several hours to finish their meals.

AGE: The age of the horse will have a definite bearing on its marketing value. A Thoroughbred weanling destined for a racing career will usually sell for less than a Thoroughbred yearling. More time and expense is involved in developing a weanling into a racehorse than a yearling. Most Thoroughbreds perform at their peak between the ages of 3 and 5 years.

Development of the Thoroughbred

Most professional horse people will seek a horse that is best suited for racing at a realistic price. Too many people waste their valuable time and money searching for that champion racehorse at a bargain price. There are many examples of inexpensive Thoroughbreds that were overlooked for one reason or another but went on to become champion racehorses. Such individuals include Seabiscuit, John Henry, Carry Back, Seattle Slew, and many more. However, these individuals are considered to be the exception rather than the rule. By adhering to the selection characteristics described herein, both the professional and novice horse person can accurately determine a horse's racing potential and improve their chances of locating and purchasing a horse suitable for a successful racing career.

The making of a Thoroughbred into a racehorse involves many stages of development. The first stage of development is the foal, or suckling, period. A suckling is a foal (colt or filly) that is with its dam and still nursing. Thoroughbreds are not born knowing what is expected of them as racehorses. The Thoroughbred must be properly trained and taught from birth in order to perform as a racehorse. Soon after birth, the foal is fitted with a head halter (harness) and handled daily by the attendant. The foal is then taught to lead and be caught while it is still with its dam going to and from the pasture each day. When the foal is a few days old, it is lightly groomed with a soft brush, and its feet are picked clean daily. Most Thoroughbred mares do an excellent job of producing milk for their nursing foals. In order for the foal to grow and develop, many farms will begin feeding a month-old foal about a quart of grain daily. This amount is in addition to the mare's milk that is consumed by the foal each day.

Feed consumption is an excellent indicator of the general health of the foal. If a foal doesn't eat its daily grain ration, it is a good sign that the foal may have a low-grade infection or be anemic. A normal foal ration consists of high-quality oats and has a 20% protein level.

The second stage of development is the weanling period. A weanling is a foal (colt or filly) under 1 year of age that has been weaned from its dam and is no longer nursing. On most Thoroughbred breeding farms, the foals are separated from their dams during the fall at about 5 to 6 months of age. The process of weaning can be very traumatic for both mare and foal. Tranquilizers may be administered to the mare and weanling to reduce the trauma of separation. On a designated day, the mares are lead off to another part of the farm where they are unable to hear their foals and physical contact is impossible. The weanlings are placed in stalls in a training barn, and each day they are turned out into separate paddocks according to their sex. It sometimes takes a few days for the weanlings to settle down and begin eating satisfactorily. Weanlings are fed about 10 to 12 pounds of hay and 10 to 12 quarts of grain per day. By the time the foals become weanlings, they should be familiar with leading, grooming, and having their feet handled and cleaned. The weanlings are taught to be tied to the stall wall and to stand quietly while they are being groomed. A rubber tie strap and head halter is used for this task. Weanlings usually receive a more thorough grooming than that of a foal. The entire grooming procedure lasts about 15 minutes for each weanling. The feet of the weanlings are trimmed about once a month by the black-smith. The weanlings are usually turned out in large paddocks or pastures throughout the winter and spring. It is during this time that each horse learns of its position, or ranking, within the herd.

Each day the weanlings play, graze, and develop mentally and physically. The game ones exhibit their competitiveness at the weanling stage of their lives. One can easily observe their competitive spirit in the paddocks and pasture when they are running, rearing, and playing. At the end of the day when its time to come into the barn, the good ones will make an extra effort to be first to the gate of the paddock or pasture. One of the most important periods in the life of a Thoroughbred is the yearling stage. A yearling is a young horse (colt or filly) between 1 and 2 years of age. It is during the yearling stage that the Thoroughbred is introduced to a saddle, bridle, and rider. All Thoroughbreds become a year older on January 1 of each year. It is the universal birthday of all Thoroughbreds, regardless of the actual birth date of the individual Thoroughbred. This date is a result of the early development of the Thoroughbred in England. In seven-teenth-century England, the racing season ended in late fall and did not resume again until spring, therefore, the logical time to change the age of all Thoroughbreds was during this break in the racing season. However, recent changes in Thoroughbred racing have made this date impractical. Year-round racing in the United States has made January 1 simply a date for all Thoroughbreds to become one year older.

Thoroughbred Training

The yearling is usually introduced to saddle, bridle, and rider starting around August or September, and this lasts for a peri-od of about 60 to 75 days. Yearlings are usually sent to farms and training centers throughout the world for their initial training. The Thoroughbred must be trained properly in order to become a racehorse. Their first lessons include the acceptance of the saddle, bridle, and rider. By August of the Thoroughbred's yearling season, it is actually 15 to 20 months of age and weighs approximately 800 to 1,000 pounds. Yearlings must be handled gently and with a great deal of patience. They are just like children; some learn faster than others, but each yearling must be allowed to learn at its own pace. They are creatures of habit, and they don't forget much, good or bad.

The basic training process varies with individuals but usually consists of the following steps.

STEP 1. BASIC STALL WORK: The feed tub and water bucket are removed from the stall before the lesson begins. A head halter with a chifney bit is used to simulate a bridle and to get the horse used to having a bit in its mouth. The chifney bit is attached to the halter, and a lead strap is attached to the lower ring of the chifney bit and halter in order to control the horse from the ground (Figure 3-2). The horse is then taught to walk in a circle in the stall in both directions by the handler.

The next step is the introduction of the saddle pad and surcingle. The saddle pad is placed on the horse's back, and an elastic surcingle is placed over the pad and loosely attached around the heartgirth area (Figure 3-3). Once the saddle pad and surcingle are in place, the handler again moves the horse in a circular direction in the stall in both directions. When the horse becomes accustomed to the saddle pad and surcingle on its body, the elastic surcingle is then tightened. At this point the horse may begin to buck, so it is important to keep the horse moving at a walk in both directions in the stall. It usually takes about 10 days to reach this point.

Bellying the horse by the rider is the next step after the horse is used to the saddle pad and elastic surcingle. The rider

3-2. A head halter with a chifney bit is used to simulate a bridle and to get the horse used to having a bit in its mouth. (Author)

now enters the stall with the handler, and the handler assists the rider to lie across the back of the horse, or to belly the horse (Figure 3-4). As the rider is lying across the back of the horse on his/her belly, the handler again moves the horse forward at a walk in both directions. The yearling now feels the weight of a rider on its back for the first time. As soon as the horse accepts the weight, it is time for the rider to place a leg on each side of the horse and straddle the horse's back, sitting in an

upright position. The rider will usually ease quietly off the horse to the ground and get back up again on the horse's left side. The procedure for mounting and dismounting is repeated several times on the first day.

The next step is to carefully place the bridle on the head. Here a D snaffle bit replaces the chifney bit and is placed in the horse's mouth. The bridle is usually placed on the head over the halter (Figure 3-5).

Once the yearling has accepted the saddle pad, elastic surcingle, bridle, and rider, it is time for the saddle and girth, which replace the saddle pad and elastic surcingle. For a period ranging from 7 to 14 days, both horse and mounted rider walk in a circle in both directions inside the stall for about 15 minutes each day. The handler will wait outside the stall ready to assist the rider in the event of an emergency. The handler will also assist in placing and removing the equipment as well as helping the rider mount each day.

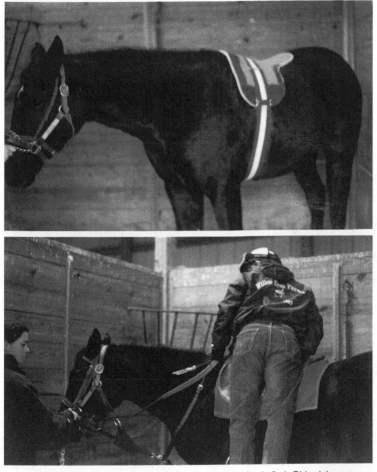

3-3. The saddle pad and elastic surcingle in place (top). 3-4. Rider lying across the back of the yearling to allow the horse to feel weight for the first time while being moved back and forth (below). (Author)

STEP 2. OUTSIDE STALL WORK: After the basic stall work is completed, it is time to move the training work to outside the stall.

Each day, the yearling is equipped with a saddle, bridle, and rider and led around the aisle of the barn by a handler. The handler will lead the yearling and rider until the horse is

3-5. The bridle is carefully placed on the head and a D snaffle bit replaces the chifney bit. (Author)

accustomed to the rider and its surroundings (Figure 3-6).

When the yearling and rider are walking quietly, the handler steps away, and horse and rider are on their own. Each day, the yearling is jogged with the other horses in a single file for about 5 minutes, walked, and then jogged again. All this is performed in the aisle or a confined area of the barn. For the next few days, the jogging time is increased, and the horse is made to go in both directions.

After the yearling has worked up to jogging a mile in both directions, it is taught to back up and stand quietly with the rider.

Now the horse is ready to go to a paddock or an open field. Here the yearling is taught to jog in both directions and then made to jog in a figure-8 pattern. Once the yearling has mastered the figure-8 pattern at a jog, it is ready for a faster pace called the canter. A canter is a gait that is merely a slow, restrained gallop. The yearling is then jogged and cantered in the paddock for approximately 10 days.

The yearling is now ready to go to the training track. Some farms and training centers will have a starting gate on the track, and the yearlings are permitted to walk past the gate on their way to and from the track. The yearlings are taught to stand or walk through the open gate to allow them to become accustomed to the starting gate.

As training progresses, each yearling must learn to run on the inside, outside, and between horses, just as they would during an actual race. Three weeks after the yearlings have

3-6. A yearling, equipped with a saddle, bridle, and rider, is led around the barn by a handler. This will continue each day until the horse is accustomed to the rider and its surroundings. (Author)

started cantering on the training track, the training distance is increased to approximately a mile and a half per day.

Any bad experiences during a yearling's early training can affect its future as a racehorse. Bringing a horse to the point of maximum fitness slowly allows the feet, ligaments, tendons, and joints to become accustomed to the stress placed upon them and to adapt themselves to withstand the rigors of racing.

STEP 3. RACE TRAINING: All the yearlings become 2 year olds on January 1. At this point, some yearlings are merely turned out daily in a pasture for the remainder of the winter to allow them to grow and mature until spring. Others are shipped to trainers at various racetracks to begin their conditioning and race training.

It is at the racetrack that the trainer will get the 2 year olds conditioned for actual racing. This includes developing a horse's speed, stamina, and ability to break from the starting gate. Each Thoroughbred must be schooled in the mornings to properly break from the starting gate by the official starter (Figure 3-7). Each horse must be able to stand quietly inside the starting gate; back out of the gate in the event that there is a problem at the start of a race; alertly break from the gate, first alone and then with company; and alertly break from the gate with company to the sound of a ringing bell.

Upon fulfilling the above requirements in several morning schooling sessions, the official starter will approve a horse from the gate and issue a gate card to the trainer that allows the horse to be officially entered into a race at any racetrack in the country. On the other hand, if a horse fails to enter or leave the starting gate or behaves badly in the gate in an official race, then the horse is automatically placed on the starter's list and is not permitted to race until it is reapproved from the starting gate.

Thoroughbred Identification

Before a horse is permitted to race, its identity must be developed and verified by the official identifier at the racetrack. The function of the identifier's office is to be certain that each horse entered into a race is in fact the same horse that runs.

3-7. Each Thoroughbred must be schooled in the mornings to properly break from the starting gate by the official starter. (Author)

In years past, many unscrupulous owners and trainers would substitute a fast ringer to replace a mediocre runner. It is now required by the owner or trainer to submit the original Jockey Club foal certificate to the racing identification office upon the horse entering the racetrack grounds. The foal certificate remains in the custody of the identifier's office until the horse officially leaves the racetrack grounds. Each racetrack shall require the original Jockey Club foal certificate to be placed on file before a horse is permitted to race.

The following information is found on each and every foal certificate issued by the Jockey Club of America:

Registration number
Name of owner
Name of horse
Name of breeder
Color of horse
Complete head and leg markings
Pedigree (sire and dam)
Racing record

The official Jockey Club Thoroughbred color guide consists of the following:

BAY: The most common color of Thoroughbreds. It varies from yellow to tan to bright auburn; the mane and tail are always black.

BLACK: The entire body coat, including muzzle, flanks, and legs are black.

BROWN (dark bay): There are tan hairs on the muzzle and/or flanks; the mane and tail are always black.

CHESTNUT: The color is yellow-red to red-yellow to a golden yellow. Mane and tail are the same color as the body coat.

GRAY: Most of the body coat is a mixture of black and white hair.

ROAN: Most of the body coat is a mixture of red and white hair.

WHITE: The entire body coat is white, including the mane and tail.

In addition to the Jockey Club foal certificate, each Thoroughbred must be tattooed before they are permitted to race. The identifier's office will arrange for a horse to be lip tattooed when the horse is on the racetrack grounds and is ready to race. The tattoo is placed on the inside of the upper lip. It is a quick procedure in which the tattoo technician merely presses an inked needle plate against the inside of the upper lip. No tattoos are alike; each Thoroughbred has its own individual tattoo for the rest of its life (Figure 3-8).

The tattoo consists of a letter and 4 or 5 numbers (e.g., A 12345). The letter represents the year the horse was born (e.g., A = 1997). The numbers represent the last 4 or 5 digits of the Jockey Club foal certificate registration number. For example, if the Jockey Club foal certificate registration number is 9581234, then the numbers 1234 are used for the tattoo. Finally, the identifier requires actual photographs of each horse stabled on the racetrack. These photographs identify the horse's color, head and leg markings, scars, etc. The photographs are taken by the staff of the identifier's office. The color photographs consist of front and side views of the horse and are used before each race to verify the horse's identity.

Once the Thoroughbred begins its racing career, it will eventually find its level of competition where it is most successful. The trainer will evaluate the horse's racing ability, and it will continue to

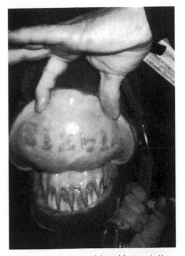

3-8. Each Thoroughbred has a tattoo under its upper lip indicating the year the horse was born and its registration number. (Author)

compete at a level where it is best suited to win. A racehorse is considered to be a maiden if it has never raced or it has raced but has never won. During a Thoroughbred's racing career, it may compete on many different levels. Horseracing may be broken down into four basic types of races.

CLAIMING RACE: A race in which each horse entered is eligible to be purchased at a specific price.

ALLOWANCE RACE: A race in which the racing secretary sets certain conditions to determine the weights assigned to each horse based on sex, age, and past performance.

HANDICAP RACE: A race for which the racing secretary or track handicapper assigns weights to each horse based on past performances.

STAKE RACES: A race in which the owner must pay a fee in order to enter and race a horse. Fees are required for nominating a horse, entering the horse, and eligibility to start the horse.

For a detailed description of the various types of races, refer to chapter 12.

The Thoroughbred racehorse is a unique animal in that it possesses a strong competitive spirit. It is capable of reaching speeds of up to 40 miles per hour and can have a single stride of over 20 feet. The Thoroughbred is not only the fastest of all horse breeds over a 1/4 mile, but is considered by many naturalists to be the fastest animal in the world over distances of 1 mile or more. The Thoroughbred runs because it wants to run—because running is simply a fulfillment of its physical design.

4

PHYSICAL CONDITIONING OF THE RACEHORSE

Now that you are familiar with the general composition of the racetrack, the professionals that make up the sport, and the types and early development of racehorses/Thoroughbreds, let us now focus on the racing horse, the heart of the industry. Most horses go through cycles in their training; that is to say, they have peaks and valleys. It is the duty of the bettor to determine whether the horse is improving or declining. Naturally a horse in top physical condition will run a good race. The horse in poor physical condition will more than likely turn in a poor performance. Wagering on a horse in poor condition is a waste of money.

There are some horses that are forced to race even though they may not be physically up to the task at hand. A trainer may be pressured by the owner(s) to race the horse, and if the trainer doesn't oblige the owner, the trainer may lose the owner as a client. Even the racing office will sometimes ask a trainer to fill a race with a horse that may not be quite ready to run. Sometimes a race comes up short of entries, and in order to utilize the race as part of the program the next day, more horses must be recruited by the racing office to fill the race.

In some states, a minimum of 5 horses is required to start in a race in order to offer exotic wagering such as exacta or quinella. If a trainer fails to comply with the wishes of the racing office, then the trainer may risk not being granted stalls at the next racing meet. Without stalls on the racetrack grounds, the trainer's economic livelihood may be in jeopardy. Other factors may also contribute to a racehorse's poor condition such as a low-grade infection, weight loss, respiratory distress, loss of appetite, time lapsed between races, poor nutrition, poor shoeing, and minor musculoskeletal problems. Some of these factors may not be evident to the trainer, and therefore the horse is entered into a race and expected to perform at its best.

There are two basic methods of getting a horse into good physical condition. They are through rigorous training or through actual racing. Most horses rarely maintain their best form for more than a 6-week period. If a horse is absent from competition for 30 days or more, it is usually put through a series of workouts for the sole purpose of getting into peak condition. Since it is virtually impossible for the bettor to collaborate with the trainer of each horse concerning his or her condition, it would be wise for the bettor to become familiar with *The Daily Racing Form* publication. *The Daily Racing Form* is a bargain at a cost of $5.00 when one considers the amount of information provided on each horse entered on any given day at any racetrack in the United States and Canada. From novice to professional handicapper, *The Daily Racing Form* is an essential tool for everyone attending the races.

The Daily Racing Form will provide the bettor with all the information required in order to determine the capability of each horse in a race (Appendix C, How to Read *The Daily Racing Form*). The physical condition of a horse can be determined by utilizing the result charts appearing in the past performances section of *The Daily Racing Form*. By consulting the latest result charts and following the running lines of each horse, it is a simple task to note the progress (or lack of it) as each race unfolds from beginning to end.

Workouts are often valuable in determining the overall physical condition of the horse. The frequency of the workouts is more important than the time of each workout.

Training may consist of long, slow gallops of 2 or more miles each day followed by short, stringent speed drills. This method of training will generally tighten up the muscles of a horse, which may have lost tone due to idleness. This type of training may also improve breathing and aid in the development of stamina as well as increasing speed and contributing to the overall physical condition of the horse.

Recent performances will usually reveal signs of a horse approaching a winning form. They may include the following:

A horse has shown early speed in a race where it previously did not.

There is evidence of a burst of closing speed late in a race or at the end of a morning workout.

The ability of a horse to come on a second time during a race is sure sign of a horse approaching peak form.

When horses begin to lose their winning form, they frequently continue to illustrate evidence of speed in several races but not enough in order to win. In other words, each display of speed lasts for a shorter period of time as the horse retreats from a winning form.

Another indication of a horse losing its winning form is that it shows a continuous pattern of poor performances, especially after a drop in class. If a horse has not raced within 30 days or more, the bettor should conclude that there is a definite reason for the layoff. Most likely the horse was laid up for some physical abnormality.

Remember, top-quality stake horses race about once every 30 days but are able to hold their winning form for a longer period of time than claimers and allowance horses. In addition to the performance record, physical condition is equally important and can tell you a great deal about a horse's chances of running a good race.

When you are physically at the racetrack, there are 2 areas that are considered best to view the physical condition of each

4-1. The saddling paddock is the best area to evaluate the physical condition of each horse in a race. It is also another way to fully enjoy the experience of being at a racetrack. (Author)

horse in a race. They are the saddling paddock and the post parade. The saddling paddock is the area at the racetrack where each horse is saddled by its trainer before each race (Figure 4-1). At the saddling paddock, the betting public is able to observe the horses close up. Many race goers remain in the grandstand or clubhouse and neglect to take the opportunity to visit the saddling paddock. The post parade is the period of time when the horses leave the saddling paddock and make their way to the starting gate. During the post parade, each horse is paraded in front of the grandstand at a walk in numerical order and then is allowed to warm up at a gallop or trot.

The saddling paddock is the best area for the bettor to evaluate the physical condition of each horse in a race. It is also another way to fully enjoy the experience of being at a racetrack. When viewing the horses in the saddling paddock, your first area of concern is the condition of the horse's coat.

4-2. Horses that are in top physical shape will exhibit light and dark spots called dapples on the sides of their bodies. (Author)

The coat should be gleaming and shiny as opposed to being dull. A bright, glistening coat is a sure sign that the horse is receiving excellent care and nutrition and is in top physical shape. A shiny coat is the first thing to go when a horse becomes ill and the last thing to return when it becomes healthy. Horses that are in top physical shape will exhibit light and dark spots called dapples on the sides of their bodies. These dapples are produced internally within the skin and not in the hair coat. A horse must be in top physical condition in order to produce a dappled coat appearance (Figure 4-2).

Another area of concern is the muscling exhibited by each horse. Good muscling is necessary for a good performance. The front of the horse should exhibit well-muscled forearms, shoulders, and chest. The rear portion of the horse should display heavy muscling on the inside and outside areas of the gaskins. Gaskin refers to that area of the hind leg found between the stifle and the hock joints. The tibia and the fibula are the bones of the gaskin. The hind legs are the propelling

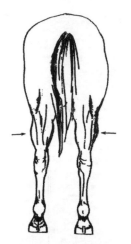

4-3. Gaskin is the area of the hind leg between the stifle and the hock joints (arrows) and should display heavy muscling. (Author)

force behind each stride, therefore, well-muscled gaskins are a must (Figure 4-3).

A racing dimple is a crease within the rear muscle tissue extending from the gaskins to the tail head. If a horse has a racing dimple on each side of its hindquarters, it is a sure sign that the horse is in top physical shape (Figure 4-4). The more horses you observe and compare, the more proficient you will become in determining the overall physical condition of a horse. During the period when the horses are in the saddling paddock, you should also observe their behavior as an aid in determining their overall condition. A well-conditioned horse should be responsive to its handlers, have its ears pricked, and be alert and responsive to the activity of the crowd. During the post parade, it should move fluently at the trot and canter. Take note of how the racehorse reacts to its escort pony. If it is playful and aggressive toward the pony, this is a good sign that the racehorse is anxious and ready to run.

A horse that is frightened will tend to grind its teeth, swish its tail, rear up, throw its head high in the air, move about constantly, and show the white around the eyes. A frightened horse is more likely to break into a sweat while in the saddling area. The frightened horse should not be confused with the angry horse. The angry horse will move its tail in an up and down motion, pin its ears back against its head, stomp its feet, and may kick out with its hind legs. Both the angry and frightened horse will use up a great deal of energy that should be used during a race. It is also important to observe each horse during the post parade. A frightened or angry horse will display the same behavior patterns during the post parade as it did in the saddling area. If a horse is eager to run, both hind feet will hit the ground at the same time while it is warming up with an escort pony. The rider on the escort pony will have a tight hold of the eager horse, causing it to hold its head high. A horse will sometimes arch its neck and head due to the tight hold of the jockey during the post parade. This is a good sign that the horse is on the bit and is ready to put in a good effort. While the horses are being paraded in front of the grandstand, it is important to observe their walk.

4-4. A racing dimple on each side of the hindquarters (arrow) is a sure sign that the horse is in top physical shape. (Author)

A horse that is prancing as opposed to walking is showing a sure sign of eagerness. A horse will sometime drag its hind feet during the walk. This is noted by dirt being kicked up during the walk. A horse that drags its feet at the walk certainly will lack the coordination and agility required to perform well during the high speed of racing.

The appearance of sweat on a horse before a race either in the post parade or the saddling paddock is not a good sign. There are many reasons for a horse sweating prior to a race. Obviously if the air temperature is high and it is a humid day, a horse will sweat in order to maintain its normal body temperature (which is approximately 100 degrees F), but a nervous or frightened horse will also begin to sweat regardless of temperature. Finally, if a horse is ill, it may also break into a sweat, however, illness should not be a consideration on race day. On race day, each horse is examined by a veterinarian appointed by the state racing commission to determine the horse's physical ability to race. If a horse shows evidence of a fever or a low-grade infection, it will be declared scratched from the race by the veterinarian.

Sweating usually begins as dark spots on the belly and flanks. Sweat takes on a foamy texture when rubbing occurs. Foam may develop between the hind legs due to the inner thighs rubbing. Foam may also develop on both sides of the neck from the reins rubbing the neck area. If a horse is wearing a breastplate, foam may develop on the chest area. When a horse is dripping sweat, the horse is said to be washed out. If a horse becomes washed out prior to a race, it's a sure sign that the horse will not perform well. It is normal for a horse to sweat after a race due to exertion, especially in hot, humid weather.

The observer must also be aware of the opposite of profuse sweating—a condition called anhidrosis. Anhidrosis, or dry coat, is the loss of the horse's ability to sweat. Racehorses shipped in from temperate areas to hot, humid areas are susceptible to this condition. A horse with anhidrosis will not exhibit any signs of sweating anywhere on the body. The coat will appear rough and dull and will remain dry before and after a race or workout. Horses bred and raised in hot, humid areas very rarely develop anhidrosis. The cause of this condition is uncertain, but is believed to be associated with low levels of sodium and chloride in the blood. Horses suffering from this condition will exhibit symptoms such as an elevated pulse and respiration rate and a core body temperature of 105–108 degrees F if stressed due to hard work. Excessive amounts of urine may also be a symptom of this condition. In severe cases of anhidrosis, a horse may collapse and go into cardiac arrest after a race or workout. If the horse has this condition, it is best to avoid racing in hot, humid areas, as it will have an affect on a horse's performance.

Once a racehorse reaches its top physical condition, a trainer may apply various types of equipment to the horse in order for it to maintain its level of fitness for a long period of time.

RACING EQUIPMENT AND MEDICATIONS

Racing equipment has a definite bearing on a horse's ability to race. It is important that the racing fan understand the significance of racing equipment and how it is utilized.

The best area to view the equipment worn by each horse is when the horses are in the saddling paddock prior to a race. It is here that the racing fan can easily view each horse close up and determine the type of equipment worn. Standard equipment for all racehorses to race and train includes a saddle and bridle.

Additional racing equipment may be used to protect a horse from injury, to give the horse better traction, to correct a bad habit, or to help the horse to focus during a race. In addition to the racing saddle and bridle, the racing equipment that is commonly used on racehorses includes nosebands, blinkers, racing bits, and racing plates (horseshoes).

Nosebands

The primary purpose of the noseband (sometimes called a caveson) is to keep the mouth of the racehorse in a closed position during a race or exercise. By keeping the horse's mouth closed, the rider has better control over the horse. It also prevents the horse from playing with the bit with its tongue. The noseband is considered by most horse people to be part of the bridle and is placed on the horse before the

45

horse enters the saddling paddock. Not all horses require the use of a noseband. However, many racehorses require its use for top performance.

There are various types of nosebands that are commonly used on racehorses. The most common types of nosebands are the standard, the figure-8, the shadow roll, and the hinged or flash noseband.

STANDARD NOSEBAND: This type of noseband may be adjusted high or low by the buckle located on the left cheek strap of the noseband. The standard noseband should be fitted about 1 or 2 inches below the horse's protruding cheekbones to properly secure the mouth in a closed position (Figure 5-1).

FIGURE-8 NOSEBAND: The figure-8 noseband is so named because it resembles the number 8. A figure-8 noseband is useful on a horse that constantly plays with its tongue and gets its tongue over the bit. It is fastened by one strap buckled under the jaw and by another strap buckled in front of the bit under the chin. A third strap is fastened behind the ears, and a round disc lies on the bridge of the nose to protect it from the pressure of the adjustment straps (Figure 5-2).

FLEECE SHADOW ROLL: While a shadow roll serves to keep the horse's mouth closed like any noseband, its most important function is to prevent the horse from spooking at shadows during a race or workout. Shadow rolls prevent the horse from seeing shadows, wet spots, or dirt clods directly in its path or to the sides. Horses that attempt to dodge or jump over shadows during a race are likely to lose valuable strides or even injure themselves. The standard shadow roll is made of fleece and is frequently used on horses racing on dirt or turf (grass) courses. Its main function is to prevent distraction (Figure 5-3).

HINGED OR FLASH NOSEBAND: The hinged noseband is designed to work in a similar fashion as the figure-8 noseband. Some professional horse people believe it is more comfortable than the figure-8 noseband. The standard noseband is converted to a hinged noseband by adding a connective strap to the center of the nosepiece of the standard noseband. A second strap is then threaded through the loop formed by the connective strap and fastened with the use of a small buckle in front of the bit (Figure 5-4).

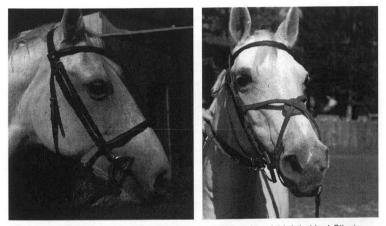

5-1. Standard noseband (left). 5-2. Figure-8 Noseband (right). (Joel Silva)

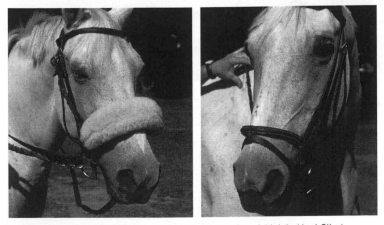

5-3. Fleece shadow roll (left). 5-4. Hinged noseband (right). (Joel Silva)

Blinkers

Blinkers are special hoods with cups fitted over part of the horse's eyes that restrict what the horse is able to see to the sides and rear. They are commonly used to correct a variety of problems affecting performance. For example, some horses shy or react negatively to other horses that approach them from behind in a race. Others prefer to stay with a pack of horses instead of moving out in front of them. Neither practice results in a winning performance.

Blinkers are usually made of nylon hood with 2 openings for the ears and plastic cups around the eye openings. On

racehorses, they are placed on the head over the bridle, but the side flaps are placed under the cheek pieces of the bridle before they are fastened under the jaw with Velcro tabs (Figure 5-5). The trainer decides if a horse requires the use of blinkers

5-5. Blinkers are special hoods with cups fitted over part of the horse's eyes that restrict what the horse is able to see to the sides and rear. (Joel Silva)

and the type of cups to be used. Some trainers will cut a small opening in the back of both eyecups to enable the racehorse to see other horses coming up from behind on a limited basis. The theory behind this practice is that seeing another horse moving up from behind will provoke the racehorse to dig in and go faster. Most racehorses are led to the saddling paddock with their bridles and blinkers already on before they are saddled. Some of the most common types of blinkers used on racehorses are the standard cup; the extended, or scoop, cup; the French cup; and the closed cup.

STANDARD-CUP BLINKERS: On standard-cup blinkers, both cups are of equal size. They are available in various cup sizes (quarter cup, half cup, and full cup) according to how much vision is to be limited. For instance, a full cup would restrict the horse's vision more than a half cup (Figure 5-6).

EXTENDED-CUP, OR SCOOP-CUP, BLINKERS: This type of blinker usually has one full cup and one extended, or scoop, cup. The extended cup is used on horses that tend to drift in or out

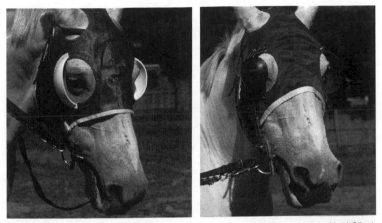

5-6. Standard-cup blinkers (left). 5-7. Extended-cup blinkers (right). (Joel Silva)

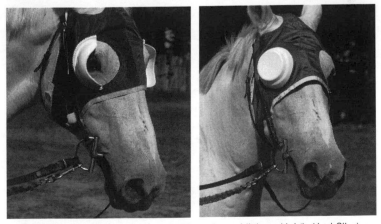

5-8. French-cup blinkers (left). 5-9. Closed-cup blinkers (right). (Joel Silva)

during a race. For example, a trainer may use an extended cup on the right eye of a horse that has a habit of drifting wide toward the outside rail (Figure 5-7).

FRENCH-CUP BLINKERS: The French-cup blinker allows the horse to see more than the full-cup blinker. The center edge of the cup is cut away in a half circle to allow a greater range of vision for the horse (Figure 5-8).

CLOSED-CUP BLINKERS: This type of blinker is used on race-horses that are blind or partially blind in the right eye. The good left eye is open with no cup at all. The closed cup protects the sensitive blind eye from flying dirt clods during a race (Figure 5-9). Most racing jurisdictions in the United States will not allow a horse that is blind in the left eye to race. Horses race in a counterclockwise direction in the United States, and if sight is impaired in any way in the left eye, the horse would be unable to see the inner rail, which would create an unsafe situation.

Racing Bits

The bit is the part of the bridle that is inserted into the horse's mouth. The purpose of the bit is to allow the jockey to control the horse before, during, and after a race. Another function of the bit is to allow the jockey to steer the horse in order to keep the horse on a straight course during the running of a race. The most common bits used on racehorses are the snaffle bit, the ring bit, and the run-out bit.

SNAFFLE BIT: The snaffle bit is the most popular type of bit that is used on a racehorse. This type of bit has a jointed mouthpiece attached to a movable metal ring, or D, at each end. The standard racing snaffle bit is usually made of stainless steel or aluminum. It may also be covered with rubber for horses with a sensitive mouth (Figure 5-10).

5-10. Snaffle bit. 5-11. Ring bit. 5-12. Run-out bit. (Author)

RING BIT: The purpose of the ring bit is to prevent the horse from grabbing either side of the bit with its teeth. If the horse grabs the bit, the jockey has little or no control over the horse during a race. It is generally used on horses that tend to lug in or out. Lugging refers to a horse that pulls toward the inside or outside of the track instead of maintaining a straight course (Figure 5-11).

RUN-OUT BIT: This is the most severe bit utilized to correct the problem of lugging in or out during a race. When the jockey pulls on the opposite rein, metal prongs on the bit jab the corner of the horse's mouth. When the jockey releases the tension on the rein, a metal spring allows the prongs to retract (Figure 5-12). A standard noseband is usually used with this bit to prevent the jockey from pulling the bit through the horse's mouth. It may also prevent the horse from playing with the bit with its tongue. This habit may interfere with the horse's breathing during a race.

Miscellaneous Racing Equipment

In addition to the saddle, bridle nosebands, blinkers, and bits a racehorse may be fitted with, other equipment is used in order to obtain the maximum performance. Miscellaneous racing equipment can include the following:

RUBBER BIT HOLDER
RUBBER BIT GUARDS
TONGUE TIE
BIT BURR
BREASTPLATE
FLAIR NASAL STRIPS®
RACING PLATES (HORSESHOES)

RUBBER BIT HOLDER: The rubber bit holder is used to prevent a horse from getting its tongue over the bit during a race. If a horse does get its tongue over the bit, the jockey loses control over the horse. The high-tension rubber nosepiece keeps the bit high against the roof of the mouth. It is attached to both sides of the bit and to the crownpiece of the bridle. Triple Crown winner Seattle Slew made this piece of equipment very popular with trainers back in the 1970s (Figure 5-13).

RUBBER BIT GUARDS: The main function of rubber bit guards is to protect the corners of a horse's mouth from being irritated by the bit. The corners of the mouth are very sensitive on a horse and are subject to rubbing and pinching from the bit, especially a snaffle bit (Figure 5-14).

TONGUE TIE: A large number of trainers will automatically tie a horse's tongue down to the lower jaw before a race. The purpose of tying the tongue is to prevent the horse from playing with its tongue and getting it over the bit during a race or workout. A tongue tie may be made of rubber bands, nylon strips, or a cloth strip. A clean cloth strip about 1 inch wide and about 24 inches long is the most common type of tongue tie (Figure 5-15).

BIT BURR: This piece of equipment is a rubber or leather disc with rubber points or stiff bristles set in a circular pattern on one side. It is usually used on a horse that has the habit of lugging. It is not as severe as the run-out bit. The bit burr is placed on the same side of the mouth as the side on which the lugging occurs. When the problem occurs, the rider simply pulls on the opposite rein. This action presses the bristles or

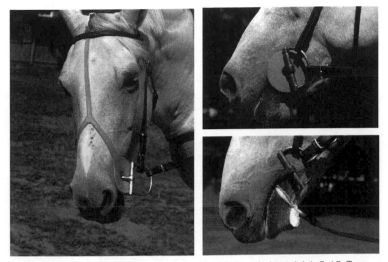

5-13. Rubber bit holder (left). 5-14. Rubber bit guards (top, right). 5-15. Tongue tie (bottom, right). (Joel Silva)

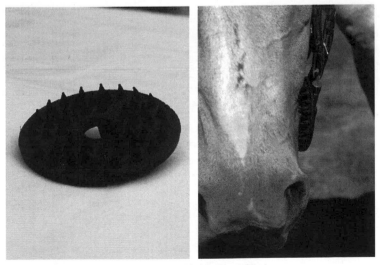

5-16. Bit burr (left); bit burr in place (right). (Joel Silva)

rubber points of the bit burr against the corner of the mouth, forcing the horse to keep a straight course (Figure 5-16).

BREASTPLATE: A breastplate is used on a racehorse to prevent the saddle from slipping back. The breastplate is attached to both sides of the girth. It is supported on the chest by a narrow strap that lies in front of the withers. Horses that have smooth, rounded withers are prime candidates to wear a breastplate. You will also find them in use on horses running in steeplechase or hurdle races. The act of jumping over obstacles may cause the saddle to slip back (Figure 5-17).

FLAIR NASAL STRIPS®: Nasal strips are designed to help racehorses breathe easier by preventing the collapse of their nasal passages. They are placed on the bridge of the nose just above the nostrils. The Flair Nasal Strips are adhered to the horse with a special medical-grade adhesive, designed for a single use. According to the manufacturer, clinical testing showed horses wearing nasal strips used 5% less energy at high speeds and during recovery. It should be noted that there are still some state racing commissions that have yet to approve their use for racing purposes (Figure 5-18).

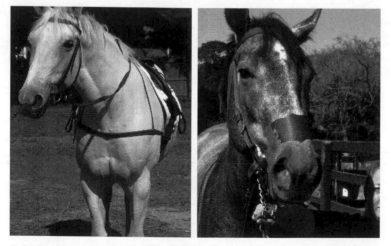

5-17. Breastplate in place (left). (Joel Silva) 5-18. Flair Nasal Strips. (Reprinted with permission of Merial Ltd. & CNS Inc.)

RACING PLATES (HORSESHOES): The most important part of the horse's body is the foot. The feet are considered to be the foundation of the entire body. There is an old adage concerning horses that states "No foot, no horse." The basic function of racing plates is to provide the racehorse with better traction and more speed. As with any athlete, racehorses wear shoes to enhance their ability to handle the various types of racing surfaces. The racing plates utilized by Thoroughbred trainers are lightweight and are made of aluminum. They are available in various sizes from the manufacturer to best fit each horse.

The job of the horseshoer (farrier/blacksmith) is to properly shape the shoe and foot for a perfect fit. The horseshoer must be sure that the feet of the horse are in perfect balance. If a horse is not properly shod, the horse may perform poorly, and serious injury may result. The following racing plates are considered to be the most common used on racehorses:

QUEEN'S PLATE

RACING PLATE WITH TOE GRAB

RACING PLATE WITH JAR/MUD CALKS

BAR SHOE

BEND SHOE

QUEEN'S PLATE: The Queen's plate is a basic aluminum shoe with no calks or grabs emanating from the ground surface of the shoe. It is merely a natural extension of the horse's hoof wall. Queen's plates are primarily used on turf runners because some racetracks do not allow the use of other types of shoes on their turf courses. Shoes with calks and grabs tend to damage the surface of a turf course (Figure 5-19).

RACING PLATE WITH TOE GRAB: This is probably the most popular shoe worn by racehorses competing on the dirt. The toe grab provides the horse with better traction. The toe grabs are available with various heights and may be worn on all 4 feet (Figure 5-20).

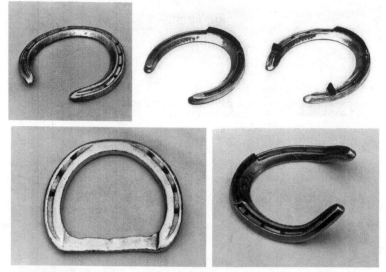

5-19. Queen's plate (top, left). 5-20. Racing plate with toe grab (top, center). 5-21. Racing plate with jar/mud calks (top, right). (Courtesy Thoro'Bred, Inc.) 5-22. Bar shoe (bottom, left). 5-23. Bend shoe (bottom, right). (Author)

RACING PLATE WITH JAR/MUD CALKS: When a racehorse is scheduled to perform on a wet or muddy racing surface, the trainer may decide to use racing plates with jar/mud calks. The calks are merely metal cleats extending from the ground surface of the shoe. There are usually 2 calks located on the heel portion of the shoe. The basic function of jar/mud calks is to provide the racehorse with better traction and stability on a wet and muddy surface. These shoes may be worn on all 4 feet (Figure 5-21).

BAR SHOE: The bar shoe is worn by horses with a thin and shallow hoof wall at the heel portion of the foot. The bar protects the sensitive heels from being stressed during a race or workout. These shoes may be worn on all 4 feet (Figure 5-22).

BEND SHOE: The use of bend shoes have become very popular with trainers in the past 10 years. Some trainers believe that the use of bend shoes on the hind feet can improve a horse's

5-24. Shoe board. The shoe board indicates the type of shoes each horse is wearing in a particular race. (Author)

performance on a dirt track. The bends provide traction and prevent a horse from slipping and sliding during a race or a workout. However, there are some professionals that feel that the use of bend shoes places stress and strain on the hind-end of a horse. Areas of stress include the back, hocks, and stifles. These shoes are usually worn on the hind feet only but may be used on the front feet as well (Figure 5-23).

The racing fan should be aware of the types of shoes worn by the horses in each race. To pick that elusive winner, the racing fan should be equipped with the knowledge as to what type of shoe fits the racing surface at hand. The announcer at the racetrack will usually announce to the general public any variation in the shoes worn by each horse in a particular race. The racing fan may also turn to the shoe board for information on shoes worn by each horse in a race. The shoe board may be found near the betting windows or on the tote board located on the infield of the racetrack. The shoe board merely indicates to the betting public the use of mud calks, bend shoes, etc. for each horse in a race (Figure 5-24).

Every racetrack employs a paddock farrier who, accompanied by a racing official, inspects the type of shoes worn by each horse in a race as they enter the saddling paddock. They inspect the shoes to determine if they are legal to use on the type of surface on which the horses are scheduled to race. At the time of entry, the trainer is required to notify the entry clerk of the type of racing plate to be used on his/her horse. Failure to do so will subject the trainer to a fine or suspension or both, depending on the circumstances.

In addition to equipment and shoes, a racehorse may be under the influence of certain drugs in order for it to perform at its best.

Racing Medication

There was a time when racehorses would race and win on just oats, hay, and water. Today, very few horses can go an entire racing season without medical treatment and the administration of medication. Some of these medications can dramatically affect the performance of a horse on the racetrack. For the average racing fan who has difficulty enough determining the abilities of a racehorse's performance without the influence of drugs, there is very little information available to illustrate what certain drugs are capable of doing.

The drugs that are commonly administered to racehorses are many. The following is a brief synopsis of the most popular drugs in use.

ANTI-INFLAMMATORY DRUGS: These relieve local swelling, redness, and pain.
CORTISONE (corticosteriod) is used to treat muscular problems such as inflammation of the muscular tissue and joints or minor strains or sprains. However, treating a horse with large doses of corticosteriods and then allowing the horse to race is

not in the best interests of the horse. This is especially true if the horse has a preexisting condition that may be worsened with excessive exercise. In cases of inflammation within a joint, injection of a corticosteriod into the joint bursa offers immediate relief from the signs of inflammation. It should be used in conjunction with rest to achieve complete healing, with a minimum loss of function around the joint.

The rules of racing in most states include the rule that no drugs may show up on prerace or postrace blood, urine, or saliva tests. Most laboratories do not bother to report corticosteriods findings, as they are similar in makeup to corticosteriods produced naturally by horses' adrenal glands. Since most corticosteriods are not stimulants or depressants, most veterinarians and racing officials feel their use should be permitted for use in racing.

A common practice on the racetrack is injecting a joint (ankle, knee, or hock) with a corticosteriod, even if it is not certain whether a horse has a bone chip or not, and then dropping the horse down in a claiming race in the hope that the horse will be claimed. Racehorses tend to suffer irreparable damage from continued injection of corticosteriods into the joints along with continued racing and training. The undesirable side effects of corticosteroids include sodium retention, potassium loss, and muscle wasting. However, the most serious side effect with long-term use of cortisone is adrenal exhaustion. Since cortisone is being artificially supplied to the horse, there is no stimulus to the adrenal glands for the natural secretion of corticosteriods.

PHENYLBUTOZONE (also called bute or butazolidin) is an analgesic (pain-killing), fever-reducing, and anti-inflammatory agent. It is generally thought to be most effective in conditions involving bone and joint pain. It is a very well known drug because it has been frequently detected in drug tests on the racetrack and has resulted in some disqualifications in famous races. The use of phenylbutozone became evident to the general public in the 1968 Kentucky Derby. The official winner Dancer's Image was disqualified from first place by the Kentucky State Racing Commission after the drug butazolidin was detected in a urine sample.

Studies have shown that phenylbutozone can be toxic to horses when administered in doses greater than what the manufacturer recommends. Horses that have regularly received phenylbutozone commonly have stomach ulcers. In horses the drug may be used in any painful condition associated with the musculoskeletal system. One of the main features of phenylbutozone is that it allows for the restoration of mobility, which in turn allows for the improvement of blood circulation in the affected area. It may have a dramatic effect on lameness, but only during the time period that the drug is being administered, thus illustrating that its effect is one of temporary pain relief rather than permanent cure.

DIURETICS: these cause an increase in the production and excretion of urine.

FUROSEMIDE (Lasix) is used to reduce bleeding from the capillaries within the lungs and nasal passages. As a diuretic, it reduces blood pressure by eliminating excess fluids from the body. Exercise-induced pulmonary hemorrhage (EIPH) is the diagnosis when there is evidence of bleeding from the nasal passages after a race or exercise and no other cause for the bleeding can be determined. A racehorse with this condition is referred to as a bleeder. Scientific evidence over the years has found that virtually all horses that are subjected to strenuous exercise tend to bleed from the nose. EIPH has been cited as the cause of poor performance in racehorses, but there is little evidence documenting the effects of EIPH on performance. However, Lasix is the most widely used medication by trainers to treat a horse known to be a bleeder. Those states that allow the use of Lasix on racehorses have certain guidelines for its use. In order for a horse to be eligible for the administration of Lasix, it must meet certain requirements.

Requirements for the use of Lasix will vary from state to state, however, the following basic rules apply in most cases for a horse to qualify for its use:

The horse has bled during a race or a workout, as determined by an endoscopic examination by the attending veterinarian (a professional licensed veterinarian in private practice hired by individual owners or trainers to provide medical treatment for their horses in training. He or she will also advise the owner and trainer on matters such as horse sales, nutrition, and training schedules).

The horse has visibly bled during a race or a workout, as determined by the state-appointed veterinarian (a professional licensed veterinarian employed by and representing the state racing commission in all matters concerning the medical treatment and well-being of all horses stabled on the grounds. Any and all drug-related treatments by attending veterinarians must be reported to the state-appointed veterinarian. The state-appointed veterinarian must also maintain a list of injured horses on the grounds as well as horses deemed ineligible for racing).

The horse has raced on Lasix in its last race in another jurisdiction with similar rules.

The horse has been qualified by a state veterinarian for the administration of Lasix in another racing jurisdiction.

A horse that has been approved for the administration of Lasix may be removed from the Lasix list, upon authorization from the stewards.

When drugs are administered to racehorses in a responsible and prudent manner by veterinarians, they are for the most part safe and do not cause any serious problems. Many owners and trainers depend on therapeutic medication in order to keep their horses in competition, but drug abuse does exist. Each state racing commission governs the drug-testing procedures used on racehorses after competition. State racing commissions vary in their rules and regulations regarding medications as they apply to racehorses. Normally, testing involves the collection of blood and urine samples from the winner of each race. Beaten betting favorites in a race are also tested as well as horses selected on a random basis. If a positive result does occur, a hearing is held by the presiding stewards with the trainer, and a penalty in the form of a suspension or a fine (or both) may be issued. The guilty horse is usually disqualified, and all purse money is forfeited and redistributed to the other owners with horses in the same race. The race is officially eliminated as part of the racing record of the horse with the positive test.

The racing fan can easily determine if a horse is racing on butazolidin or Lasix, as their use is indicated on the program as well as the past performance of each horse entered in a race. If the horse is racing on Lasix, then the letter L will appear in parentheses (L) after the horse's name. If it is racing with Lasix for the first time, then it will appear as the letter L followed by the number 1 (L1). First-time Lasix use may also be shown as (FTL). The use of butazolidin is indicated in the same manner with the letter B appearing after the horse's name.

It is important for the bettor to be familiar with the use of butazolidin and Lasix. For example, if a horse has been racing and winning with the use of drugs at a racetrack located in a state that permits the use of drugs and is then entered to race in a state that prohibits the use of drugs, then the bettor should not expect that horse to perform as it did in the past. Naturally, the opposite is true. If a horse was racing poorly in a state where the use of drugs was prohibited and is then entered in a race in a state where these drugs are legal, then the bettor can expect the horse to put in a good performance. History has shown that horses did not race with the use of performance-enhancing drugs until about 1970. Are the horse-breeding programs here in the United States producing inferior horses? If so, is drug use the answer, or should the breeder concentrate on producing a better product? These are just a few questions that must be addressed by both breeders and racing officials. The fact remains that many of the drugs administered to racehorses are legal in many states. It is highly unlikely that their use will be prohibited any time in the near future. It is sad to say, but the widespread use of drugs both legal or illegal will continue to undermine the integrity of the sport of horseracing.

When handicapping a race, the racing fan should always make note of any changes in the use of equipment or drugs, as this is an important step in selecting that eventual winner. The addition or removal of blinkers, tongue tie, nosebands, or shoes or a change in the type of drugs used are all important observations not to be overlooked. Any change in equipment or drugs utilized on a horse is a sure sign that the trainer is making every effort to obtain the best performance possible from his/her horse. In addition to the use of racing equipment, certain bandages and adhesive patches may be used to enhance a horse's racing ability.

BANDAGES AND PATCHES

It is very important to make note of the type of bandages or patches a horse is wearing in a race. Some of the most common bandages and patches worn by a racehorse are cold-water bandages, run-down bandages, vinyl run-down patches, rubber run-down patches, and felt patches.

COLD-WATER BANDAGES: It should be understood that a horse does not race in these bandages. The groom removes them from the front legs in the saddling paddock.

There are some trainers who believe that soaking a horse's front legs in ice water before a race will prevent or alleviate some of the pain, swelling, and injuries that can result from concussion and stress on the front legs during a race. The front legs are placed in a large tub of ice and cold water for 30 minutes or more before a race (Figure 6-1).

In order to preserve the cold effect on the front legs, cold-water bandages are applied after the horse is removed from the tub. These bandages are soaked in ice water and applied to the ankles, tendons, shins, and knees of the front legs. The horse is lead to the saddling paddock with the cold-water bandages on its front legs.

When you see these cold-water bandages on a horse's front legs prior to a race, you will know for a fact that the horse was standing in a tub of ice water and may be suffering from general soreness (Figure 6-2).

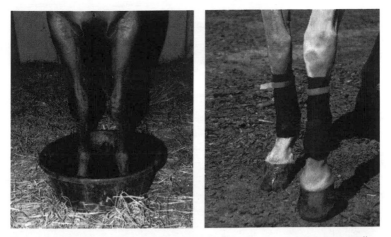

6-1. Soaking a horse's front legs in ice water before a race may prevent or alleviate swelling and injuries (left). (Gerry Mora) 6-2. Cold-water bandages indicate a horse may be suffering from soreness (right). (Joel Silva)

RUN-DOWN BANDAGES: The run-down bandage is used during a race in order to support and protect the ankles, ligaments, and tendons of all 4 legs. Running down occurs in horses that race at high speeds. Not all horses are prone to running down. When the ankles are overextended, they may come into contact with the surface of the racetrack. Since most racetracks have a sandy surface, the track becomes abrasive to the back of the ankles, and they become raw and sore. Running down is a serious problem with racehorses because the pain associated with these ankle wounds will affect a horse's performance in a race. Horses that race without run-down bandages may return from a race with blood running from the areas on the back of the ankles.

Poor conformation, fatigue, speed, and track conditions are all contributing factors to running down. Horses that have this problem usually run down on the hind ankles more so than the front ankles. A trainer usually determines whether a horse requires protection from running down based on morning workouts. Run-down bandages provide support to the ankles

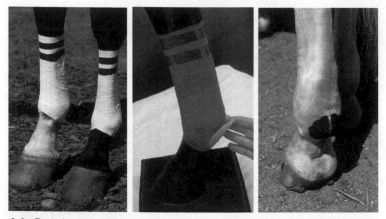

6-3. Run-down bandages (left). 6-4. Vinyl run-down patch (center). 6-5. Rubber run-down patch (right). (Joel Silva)

as well as protection. The run-down bandages may be applied solely to the ankle area, and in some cases, they are applied to the entire leg, including the ankle and cannon. The bandage will end just below the knees on the front legs and just below the hocks on the hind legs. Run-down bandages are available in various colors and are secured to the leg by a built-in adhesive and bands of electrical tape. These bandages are placed on the legs of the horse before it is led to the saddling paddock. This is to allow the horse some time to become accustomed to having bandages on its legs before the actual race (Figure 6-3).

VINYL RUN-DOWN PATCHES: The vinyl run-down patch is usually used in conjunction with a run-down bandage. It is a clear self-adhesive vinyl disc that is applied to the back of the ankle on the outside of the run-down bandage. It provides extra protection to the ankles and prevents running down. The vinyl disc is easily applied by pressing it to the back of the bandage over the ankle (Figure 6-4).

RUBBER RUN-DOWN PATCHES: This type of run-down patch is usually applied directly to the back of the ankle. There is no

need to place a run-down bandage on
the leg. The rubber run-down patch
comes with a plastic backing that is
removed to expose the adhesive.
Once the adhesive is exposed, the
patch is pressed firmly against the
back of the ankle. Rubber run-down
patches are usually applied to the
ankles of the horse before it is led to
the saddling paddock (Figure 6-5).

FELT PATCHES: The felt patch is not
used for run-down situations; it is
used on the limbs for the sole purpose

6-6. Felt patch. (Joel Silva)

of protection where bandaging is impractical. There are some
horses that have a tendency to hit themselves when running.
This condition is generally referred to as interference. For
example, the left foot may hit the inside of the opposite right
pastern. A felt patch is therefore placed on the inside of the
right pastern (Figure 6-6).

A horse with poor conformation may be prone to these
problems. The felt patch is self-adhesive and is simply applied
to the area that is need of protection. The felt patch is available in large sheets and may be cut with scissors into various
sizes to meet the needs of the individual horse.

Now that the racing fan understands the various types of
equipment, shoes, drugs, and bandages that are utilized on
racehorses, let us now discuss the physical makeup of the
racetrack.

7

TRACK CONDITION

One of the primary factors in determining the outcome of a horse race is the physical condition of the racetrack. The track superintendent determines the condition of the track. Horses, just like people, have individual preferences. Some horses prefer a dry track, while others prefer a wet track. The trainer can usually determine a horse's preference based on its efforts in previous races and morning workouts on both a wet and dry track. Some horses prefer to run on a turf course, or track, as opposed to a dirt track, while others prefer dirt to turf. Many professional horse people believe that a horse with a low heel and a flat, large foot will perform better on the turf than will a horse that does not have this hoof conformation.

The race goer should be familiar with the types of tracks and various degrees of track conditions that may occur. Most racetracks will post the track conditions on the infield tote board throughout the day.

Dirt Track

A typical cross section of a dirt track will consist of the following layers of soil, beginning at the surface:

A. 3 to 3 3/4 inches of sandy loam cushion
B. 8 to 10 inches of clay, silt, and sand base
C. Approximately 3 inches of sand for drainage
D. Natural soil

The basic dirt track conditions are listed as fast, good, slow, muddy, sloppy, heavy, or frozen.

FAST (FST): A fast track is one that is dry with firm footing. If dust appears on the surface, the track superintendent may have a fleet of watering trucks spray the track surface with water between races.

GOOD (GD): This condition describes a track that is wet but not to the degree of muddy or sloppy. After a long period of rain, the track condition may move from fast to good and then to sloppy. A description of good may also appear when a track is drying out after being muddy and gradually moving toward a fast condition.

SLOW (SL): A track that is designated as slow is one that has more moisture than a good track but not so much moisture as to be termed muddy.

MUDDY (MY): This track condition refers to the situation in which water has penetrated the surface of the track down to the base.

SLOPPY (SLY): The surface of the track may be covered with puddles of water, but the base of the track remains hard.

HEAVY (HVY): This particular track condition is not very common but may occur after a long period of muddy conditions. The surface of the track may become sticky.

FROZEN (FR): This track condition refers to a wet track that freezing air temperatures have caused to become frozen. Racing or training may be canceled due to this condition. This would occur at racetracks that offer winter racing and are located in areas subject to freezing temperatures.

Track conditions vary with each individual racetrack. This is primarily due to the makeup and the depth of the sand cushion. In addition to these two factors, one must also consider the drainage system. Usually the center of the track surface is the highest point, and the inside and outside rail are the lowest points. One can easily conclude that in the drying-out process, the center of the racetrack may be hard and fast while the inner rail of the track may still be soft and muddy. The bettor should be aware of the slow going on the inner rail on a wet track. Horses with post positions 1 through 3 may be at a slight disadvantage on a wet track. A jockey may hesitate to make a move on the inside if the inner rail is deeper and slower. It would be wise for the bettor to observe the running of a few races on a wet track to determine if in fact a horse is at a disadvantage on the inner rail.

The speed of every track varies from day to day—heavy tracks are slower than muddy tracks, and muddy is not as fast as slow; slow is slower than good, and good is not as fast as fast. Sloppy can be either faster than, slower than, or equal to fast, depending upon which racetrack you are discussing. These track conditions will definitely have a bearing on a horse's performance. Smarty Jones won the 2004 running of the Kentucky Derby on a muddy track. The off track and post position 13 had little affect on his performance, as he won by 2 3/4 lengths. Horses that have small feet tend to do better on a wet surface than do horses with big, flat feet. Some horses prefer to run with the pack behind the leaders, while others prefer to take the lead from the start and set the pace for the race. One must consider the fact that on a wet track, a horse that likes to run from behind will have mud flying in its face during the running of the race, whereas a frontrunner will not. A trainer can determine a horse's style of running simply by observing the horse's performance during races and by consulting with the jockeys after each race.

Turf Course

A typical cross section of a turf course will consist of the following layers, beginning at the surface:

A. Surface turf consisting of a mixture of rye, Kentucky bluegrass, and fescue plants
B. 8 to 10 inches of a topsoil-growing medium
C. Natural soil

The various track conditions also apply to the turf course at any given racetrack. The basic track conditions for turf and steeplechase racing are listed as hard, firm, good, yielding, soft, and heavy.

HARD (HD): The turf condition of the track is not yielding to pressure from the hooves of the horses. It is usually dry with a firm footing.

FIRM (FM): This is the condition of the turf course corresponding to fast on a dirt track.

GOOD (GD): This condition refers to a turf course that is slightly softer than a firm course. It usually consists of a resilient surface.

YIELDING (YL): This term simply refers to a condition between good and soft.

SOFT (SF): This description refers to the condition of the turf course that corresponds to a muddy condition on a dirt track.

HEAVY (HY): This term refers to the wettest possible condition of a turf course before the race is canceled on the turf and switched to the dirt.

The constant pounding of the feet, ankles, and legs on the hard surface of a dirt track while training or racing will create some degree of soreness or tenderness in the limbs. This is partially true of horses that may have a general weakness in these areas. When a horse is in pain, it will shorten its stride when contact is made by the feet on solid ground. A stinging sensation will travel upward through the horse's lower limbs, which in turn may prevent the horse from making an honest effort to win.

A dirt track is very stressful on the feet of a horse. The surface of a dirt track is primarily made up of sand, and sand can be very abrasive. Heat is created in the limbs of the horse due to this abrasive action or the friction that occurs after running on a dirt track. This will cause horses to slow down or even try to stop in an attempt to alleviate the pain associated with the heat that is generated.

Grass and mud are similar in that neither will cause heat in the feet during the running of a race. The feet and limbs remain cool, which will cause less stress on bad-legged horses. The grass or mud may have a soothing effect on the feet and limbs and may relieve general soreness.

The daily racing programs and newspapers reflect the turf record of each individual horse entered in a race. The turf record appears in addition to its overall race record of wins, seconds, thirds, and total money earned. The past performance of each entry must be reviewed thoroughly to determine if a true grass horse is now entered into a dirt race or a true dirt horse is entered into a turf race. If a horse is entered into a turf race for the first time, it is wise to review its pedigree for outstanding turf runners. It would be best to determine if the horse is coming from a family of turf runners before considering its chances in a turf race for the first time. *The Daily Racing Form* provides its readers with the Tomlinson ratings, found in the career box of the past performances of each horse. The rating figures are used to determine if a horse will perform well on a wet track or a turf track (Figure 7-1).

A good runner on the dirt does not necessarily run well on the turf. It is the exceptional horse that will excel in both dirt and turf races. Examples of this phenomenon would be Thoroughbreds like Kelso—Horse of the Year 5 straight years (1960 to 1964)—who performed well on both turf and dirt. Another was John Henry, who was voted Horse of the Year twice and won races on both turf and dirt. He was retired in 1985 at the age of 9 with a record of 39 victories in 85 starts.

Keep in mind that this is not a common occurrence with Thoroughbreds.

In addition to track conditions, the bettor should understand the role that distance plays in handicapping the outcome of a race.

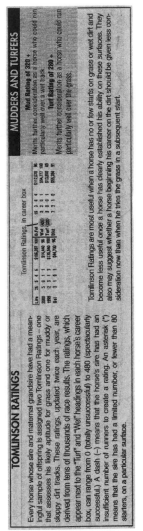

7-1. Tomlinson ratings as they appear in *The Daily Racing Form.*
(Copyright © 2003 by Daily Racing Form, Inc. and Equibase Company. Reprinted with permission.)

DISTANCE

Most racetracks in North America are oval in shape and are usually 1 mile in circumference. Smaller racetracks vary from 1/2 mile to 7/8 mile in circumference. Larger racetracks may vary in circumference from 1 1/16 miles to 1 1/2 miles. Horses race in a counterclockwise direction in the United States and Canada. A chart of a typical 1-mile racetrack is shown in Figure 8-1.

The distance of 1 mile at most racetracks is divided into 8 equal parts, each part measuring 1/8 mile. Each 1/8 mile is referred to as a furlong. Therefore, 2 furlongs will equal 2/8 or 1/4 mile. Four furlongs is equal to 4/8 or 1/2 mile. Six furlongs is equal to 6/8 or 3/4 mile (Figure 8-2). In order to accurately indicate the various distances of quarters, eighths, and sixteenths on a racetrack, poles are strategically placed around the track to represent the various distances (Figure 8-3).

Races of a mile or more are known as routes or distance races. Except for the larger racetracks (over 1 1/16 miles), route races require horses to race around 2 or more turns. A race of less than 1 mile in distance with not more than 1 turn is generally referred to as a sprint. At racetracks over 1 mile in circumference, a sprint may be as much as 7 1/2 furlongs. The most common sprint distance is 6 furlongs.

At 1-mile racetracks, sprints of 6 furlongs or higher start in a chute, which is merely an extension of the backstretch.

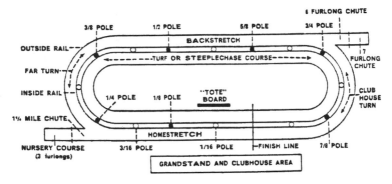

8-1. A typical 1-mile racetrack. (Author)

From the chute, the horses will run directly onto the backstretch straightway and then into the final turn, which will take them down the homestretch to the finish line.

Each 1/16 mile is equal to half a furlong. A race that is 1/16 mile more than 1 mile is simply referred to as a mile and a sixteenth (1 1/16). Races of this length allow horses more time to gain position before going into the first turn. All distances, routes, and sprints are measured from the finish line. Depending on the distance of a race, the starting point will vary on the track.

Horses that are urged for the lead in the last 2 furlongs (1/4 mile) win a large percentage of races. Horses that tend to

Distance Abbreviation	Actual Distance	Fraction of Mile
3F	three furlongs	3/8
4F	four furlongs	1/2
4½	four and one-half furlongs	9/16
5F	five furlongs	5/8
5½	five and one-half furlongs	11/16
6F	six furlongs	3/4
6½	six and one-half furlongs	13/16
7F	seven furlongs	7/8
1M	one mile	1 mile
1 1/16	mile and one sixteenth	1 1/16
1 1/8	mile and one eighth	1 1/8
1 1/4	mile and one quarter	1 1/4
1 1/2	mile and one half	1 1/2

8-2. Racetrack distances. (Author)

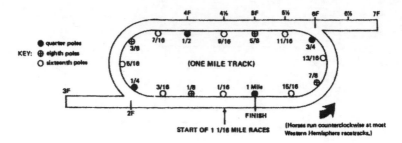

8-3. Position of poles along a racetrack indicating fractions of a mile. (Author)

win sprint races usually possess enough speed to stay close to the lead and move up on the final turn or homestretch. Horses that trail the field in the early part of sprint races usually don't finish well, much less win. Generally, a horse with an outside post position increases its chances in a distance race going around 2 turns. The inside post positions will favor horses in sprint races.

It is unusual to find a horse that is able to run well at all distances. Horses that perform poorly in both sprint and distance races are probably still searching for the distance that will best suit their mediocre ability. The ideal horse is one who has already proven its ability to run well at a particular distance. The reader should be aware of the fact that in route races, for every additional furlong run, the more the factor of weight comes into consideration. The amount of weight carried by a horse in a race is a very important factor in the handicapping process. Most of the weight carried is that of the jockey, who weighs between 100 and 115 pounds. A single pound added or deleted can make all the difference in the final outcome of a race.

When reviewing the past performance charts in the program or *The Daily Racing Form*, the bettor should take note of the following factors concerning weight:

Has the horse successfully carried the assigned weight in a previous race?

Is there an increase of 5 pounds or more since its last race?

Is the amount of weight assigned considered to be an excessive burden (120 pounds or more)?

In stake races, the weight assignments are usually uniform and are based on the age and sex of the entries. In handicap races, the racing secretary or track handicapper assigns the weights based on the horse's past performance record. A horse with a winning record will receive a higher weight than a horse with a poor winning record. In allowance races, weight assignments are based on what the entries have accomplished and the type of races that they have won. In claiming races, weights assigned depend on the value of the claiming price. The higher the claiming price, the higher the weight assigned. The number of races won and the amount of money earned also have a bearing on the amount of weight assigned to each horse.

THE TRAINER

The role of the trainer is considered by many as the most important factor when considering the success or failure of a racing stable. The *Rules of Racing* clearly states that the trainer is totally responsible for the horses in his/her care as well as the actions of his/her employees. Fines or penalties (including revocation of a trainer's license) may result from actions taken against a trainer by the official stewards of a particular racetrack.

The trainer is also responsible for making entries, declaring scratches, claiming horses, making jockey assignments, declaring fouls, and arranging for the transporting of horses. The trainer is required to set up a training schedule for each individual horse. It is the job of the trainer to prepare the horse for racing by allowing the horse to become accustomed to the starting gate and the racing and training equipment. The trainer prepares each horse with exercise in order to obtain a peak performance. The trainer supervises the grooms, hot walkers, exercise riders, jockeys, and others who provide the general care of the horse. Trainers are in contact with the owners of the horses in their care on a regular basis, keeping them informed. The modern Thoroughbred trainer will utilize a personal computer in order to e-mail his/her clients about their horses' progress. Today the personal computer is a useful tool for the trainer. With the use of a personal computer, a trainer can maintain accurate records on each horse in his/her care. Maintaining financial records concerning the overall operation of the stable is important, especially for tax purposes. Trainers of large stables may employ a professional accountant who specializes in horseracing operations to keep their financial records. Trainers have developed their own Web sites on the Internet in order to attract new clients, but it is important to understand that the more time a trainer spends on keeping track of the stable's daily operation, the less time he or she has to spend with the horses in their care.

There are basically two types of trainers: private and public. The private trainer is employed by one owner and receives a regular salary for his/her services. Private trainers are usually paid an agreed salary every month. They are usually reimbursed for any expenses incurred for the normal operation of the stable. The private trainer will generally have a part in the selection and breaking of young stock for his/her client.

The public trainer will train horses for several different owners on a per-diem basis. The rate will vary from $25.00 to over $100.00 per day. The actual rate will depend on the experience and success of the trainer as well as the geographical location of the operation. The per-diem fee will cover expenses such as labor, hay, grain, and bedding. In addition to the per-diem rate, the public trainer will also bill the owner for extra expenses, which usually include veterinary care, shoeing, special equipment, medications, and shipping fees. Both private and public trainers will receive 10% of all purse money earned by the horses in their care. They may also receive a percentage of any horse sales made on behalf of their owners.

All trainers should have a genuine love for the horse as well as patience and good horsemanship skills. Trainers come from all walks of life. Some literally grew up in the world of horseracing with backgrounds such as grooms, riders, assistant trainers, and stable hands. Others have absolutely no prior horse experience but were successful in business or some other professional endeavor. These nonprofessional trainers merely hire an assistant trainer or stable foreman to deal with the daily hands-on training of racehorses. All horses naturally know how to run, but they must be trained to utilize their natural talent in the most efficient manner.

The first skill of any trainer is to get a young horse familiar with the starting gate. It is at the starting gate where races are either won or lost. A horse may have the talent to become a winning racehorse, but all the talent in the world may not be able to overcome a poor start from the gate.

This is especially true in short sprint races. A trainer will work closely with the gate crew in order to thoroughly school a young horse in the starting gate. The horse should be able to load easily, stand quietly, back out, and break alertly. Some horses are habitually unruly in the starting gate. This behavior is usually due to poor training in the early stages of a horse's racing career. These horses must be either blindfolded or backed into the stall of the starting gate before a race.

Some horses have to be manhandled into the gate by two assistant starters who lock their arms behind the horse's hindquarters and force the horse forward into the gate (Figure 9-1). Finally, there are those horses that seem to always break slowly from the gate and are immediately at a disadvantage.

In addition to gate work, the trainer and rider must teach the horse to change its leads during a race. In North America, all racing is performed in a counterclockwise direction. The racehorse will usually lead with its left foreleg around the turns and switch to the right foreleg in the final turn and homestretch to the finish line. Most racehorses will switch their leads automatically to avoid becoming fatigued during a race, but there are those racehorses that will run the entire race on the left lead and turn in a poor performance. Some

9-1. Assistant starters lock their arms behind a horse's hindquarters and force the horse forward into the gate. This behavior may be due to poor training in the early stages of a horse's racing career. (Gerry Mora)

horses will switch leads naturally without ever being taught this maneuver by the trainer through the rider, but there are also those horses that depend on a signal from the rider. Upon entering the homestretch, the rider shifts weight and taps the horse on the shoulder with the whip in order to obtain a fluent change in leads.

The best trainers are those that are skilled at reading the condition book issued by the racing secretary and placing their horses into races where they have the best chance to win. The condition book is issued to trainers by the racing secretary's office every 10 to 14 days of a particular race meet. The condition book is actually a booklet that includes all the conditions of races, purses, and qualifications for a certain period of time of the race meet. The condition book alerts the trainer as to the type of races that are coming up for his/her consideration. Each race in the condition book specifies the date to be run, purse, length of the race, weight to be carried, and the type of horse that is eligible for entry (Figure 9-2). The condition book is written by the racing secretary and staff. In addition to stating the conditions of future races, it will include basic information such as scratch times, stable regulations, licensing information, rules of racing, and other important information.

Trainers must also have the ability to train a horse for a specific race and have that horse in the best physical condition at the time of the race. Each trainer has their own way of doing things.

There are some that stress fast workouts and others that will train their horses at a leisurely pace. Some are good with 2 year olds, while others are good with older horses. There are some trainers that do better with fillies than with colts and vice versa. Some trainers do exceptionally well with horses on the turf and become turf specialists by winning a large number of turf races. There are those that do well with horses that have speed in sprints, while others merely utilize sprint races to get a horse fit.

It is common practice among trainers to get a horse back into shape after a long layoff by actually racing the horse in a couple of races before letting the horse go all out. Sometimes a trainer will race a horse above its class to purposely lose. This poor effort will then make the horse look bad for the next race, when the horse will drop in class and go for a win with a high payoff. Trainers are considered creatures of habit

SECOND DAY - FRIDAY , MAY 7, 2000
(Entries Close on Wednesday May 5, 2000)

1 FIRST RACE	CLAIMING

Purse $ 20,000. For Fillies and Mares Four Year Olds And Upward.
Weight ....123 lbs.
Non-winners of two races at a mile or over since March 15 allowed...................... 1 lb.
Such a race since then... 3lbs.
CLAIMING PRICE $ 25,000

SIX FURLONGS

2 SECOND RACE	MAIDEN

Purse $ 44,000. For Maiden Two Year Olds.
Weight ....116 lbs.

FIVE FURLONGS

3 THIRD RACE	ALLOWANCE

Purse $ 48,000. For Three Year Olds And Upward Which Have Never Won A Race Other Than
Maiden, , Claiming, Starter Or Which Have Never Won Two Races.
Three Year Olds...117 lbs.   Older.......................124 lbs.
Non- Winners of $ 24,000 since March 15 allowed.. 2 lbs.

ONE MILE (TURF)

9-2. Page from the condition book. (Author)

and will train their horses in the same way day after day. Some trainers are more successful than others by specializing in a specific class of horse or conditions such as turf horses, two year olds, first-time starters, claiming horses, stakes and handicap horses, sprint races, and route races.

There are those trainers who are successful at certain times of the year, such as a trainer who wins a high percentage of races during the fall meet compared to the rest of the year. The racing program and *The Daily Racing Form* will print a list of trainers' standings for a current race meet. The list will include the following information on each trainer:

Number of starters to date

Number of wins, seconds, and thirds

Winning percentage (number of wins to the number of starters)

The bettor should be aware of the trainer of each horse in a race and their position on the overall trainers' standings list. The Thoroughbred racehorse is truly an athlete, and the trainer is considered to be its coach. Once you recognize the contribution of the trainer and his/her impact on a horse's performance, you are on your way to becoming a successful handicapper.

One of the most important functions of any trainer is to select a jockey for a race. Some trainers will use the same jockey on all their horses, while others will use the jockey who best fits the horse's ability. Trainers will usually select jockeys that seem to get the most out of a horse, more so than other jockeys. A trainer may select an apprentice jockey simply to take advantage of their weight allowance.

The jockey is the most visible person in the sport of horseracing, and the race goer should become familiar with the role of the jockey.

THE JOCKEY

No one individual in horseracing has more of an influence on the outcome of a race than that of the professional jockey. There are approximately 1,900 licensed jockeys in the United States. It is important for the bettor to become familiar with the jockeys riding at a particular racetrack. A jockey's performance record is a very important tool in the handicapping process. In order to decide if a jockey is suitable for a horse, the bettor should consider the following:

Whether the jockey is listed among the top 5 on the current jockey standings

Whether the jockey had a previous good race on the same horse

Whether the jockey has a high winning percentage (at least 20%)

Jockeys are considered to be some of the best athletes in the world. They must have the strength to control an animal 10 times their size as well as a keen sense of timing and quick reflexes. They must also have the ability to communicate with their mount through their hands.

Their income is derived by receiving 10% of the winner's share of the purse on winning mounts. They also receive a riding fee from $30.00 to $110.00 on losing mounts. The losing mount fees vary according to the purse structure of various racetracks. In 2003, the average earnings for jockeys from purses amounted to $49,141.00. Jockeys with 100 or more mounts in 2003 earned an average of $90,475.00, and those with 500 or more mounts in 2003 earned an average of $192,173.00 from purses.[†]

Jockeys are also responsible for incurred expenses throughout the year, such as agent fees (20% to 30% of jockey's purse earnings), valet fees (3% to 5% of jockey's purse earnings), tack and equipment, travel and meals, and union dues for the Jockey Guild ($100.00 per year, plus 5% of losing mount fees).

Some jockeys perform better on some types of horses than on others. There are those that excel in sprint races, while others perform best in distance races. Some perform their best on an off track or on a turf course. Rating a horse throughout a race is a very difficult skill for most jockeys to master. To rate a horse properly, the jockey must keep the horse off the leaders and allow the horse to settle into stride and make a move in the final stretch run. Some jockeys rely on their ability to utilize their whip during a race to get the maximum effort from their mounts. Finally, there are those riders that will purposely refrain from the use of the whip and resort to a hand ride to get the best from their mount.

It is important to understand that in distance races, it is better for the horse to carry the least amount of weight in order to maximize its chances of winning. Weight is a basic factor in all handicapping and is the only penalty available to equalize the chances of any horse in any given race. Therefore, it is important for a trainer to utilize an apprentice jockey in distance races where weight can mean the difference between winning and losing.

An apprentice jockey automatically receives a weight allowance, usually referred to as "the bug." This term was derived from the appearance of an asterisk (*) next to the

[†]Lenny Shulman, "Jockeying for Position," *The Blood Horse* (November 2004): 6,501–6,502.

apprentice jockey's name in the program and newspapers. The bug gives the apprentice jockey an allowance of 5–10 pounds as an advantage over the rest of the jockeys at a race-track. In most racing states, apprentice jockeys are allowed 10 pounds until they win 5 races. The weight allowance is then dropped to 7 pounds until they win an additional 30 races for a total of 35 wins. After 35 wins, apprentice jockeys who have not completed their first year of riding since being licensed are given an allowance of 3 pounds. When the first year is completed, they lose the bug and officially become full-fledged journeymen or journeywomen. Most jockeys weigh somewhere between 100 and 115 pounds. Part of the weight carried by jockeys includes their equipment. The total weight of the jockey's equipment will range from 2 to 3 pounds.

The jockey is responsible for providing the following equipment:

HELMET: Helmets are usually made of a durable lightweight plastic or fiberglass material. The helmet is fitted to the rider's head with a lightweight leather harness that is placed over the ears and is secured with a chinstrap and snap. All jockeys must wear a safety helmet during a race. The helmet is covered with material representing the official colors of the owner (Figure 10-1).

GOGGLES: The riding goggles are made of a clear plastic material with circular air vents on each side and an elastic strap to hold them in place over the eyes. Naturally, goggles are worn to protect the eyes of the jockey from clods of dirt being kicked up by the other horses in a race. On a wet and muddy track, a jockey may wear as many as 4 pairs of goggles. As each set of goggles becomes saturated with mud, the jockey mere-ly pulls the soiled pair downward around the neck and out of the way (Figure 10-2).

SAFETY VEST: The safety vest is required to be worn by all jockeys and consists of a lightweight foam material designed

10-1 Helmet. 10-2. Goggles. 10-3. Safety vest. 10-4. Riding breeches. 10-5. Boots. (Gerry Mora)

to provide protection and to absorb shock. It is worn on the upper body, including the shoulders. It is worn under the owner's silks. The purpose of the safety vest is to protect the rider's vital organs and ribs in the event a rider is thrown from his/her mount during a race (Figure 10-3).

RIDING BREECHES: The riding breeches, or pants, are white in color and are usually made of nylon or a similar synthetic material. The breeches are generally worn inside the boots when the track is dry and fast. There are some racing jurisdictions that now allow jockeys to display a commercial advertisement on their breeches (Figure 10-4).

BOOTS: Riding boots worn by jockeys are made of leather or a vinyl plastic with a thin heel and sole. In order to protect the boots on a wet and muddy track, the jockey will wear the breeches on the outside of the boots (Figure 10-5).

WHIP: The whip, sometimes called a crop, stick, or bat, is used by the jockey to keep the horse on a straight course and to encourage the horse to go faster and change leads during a race. The whip is made of a flexible fiberglass rod covered with dark-colored leather. At one end of the whip is a wide piece of folded leather called a popper. The whip that is generally used by most jockeys is approximately 28 inches long and weighs no more than 1 pound (Figure 10-6).

ELASTIC RACING GIRTHS: The racing saddle requires two elastic girths in order to secure it to the horse. They are referred to as an under-girth and an over-girth. The under-girth is attached to both sides of the saddle by fastening the saddle billets to each of the girth buckles. The over-girth is placed over the saddle and under-girth and is fastened to itself just behind the front legs. If these girths become worn and frayed, it is the duty of the jockey to replace them. Both girths are available in different sizes to accommodate all horses (Figure 10-7).

RACING SADDLE: The racing saddle is usually made of an inner fiberglass tree that is covered with leather or vinyl plastic. The stirrups found on each side of the saddle are usually made of aluminum. A jockey may have several different saddles depending on his/her weight assignment for a particular race. A light saddle may weigh between 1 1/2 and 2 pounds,

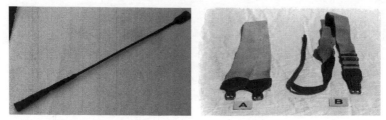

10-6. Whip (left). 10-7. Under-girth (A) and over-girth (B). (Gerry Mora)

and a heavier saddle may weigh between 3 and 4 pounds (Figure 10-8).

The colored silks and helmet cover are provided by the owner of the horse. The numbered saddlecloth as well as the back pad with pockets designed to carry lead weights are provided by the racetrack. All of the above jockey equipment is properly maintained and set out for each race by the jockey valet. Before each race, the clerk of scales must weigh each jockey and his or her equipment to be sure that each rider is carrying the assigned weight. After each race, all jockeys must be weighed out by the clerk of scales. It is possible for a jockey to lose up to 2 pounds of weight just from perspiration and physical exertion. If a jockey returns with 2 or more pounds less than their assigned weight, they may be disqualified. The loss of excessive weight (2 or more pounds) indicates that the horse failed to carry the assigned weight during the race and is therefore subject to disqualification. The jockey may be fined or suspended by the clerk of scales or another racing official in charge. Additional weight that comes from heavy rain or mud is taken into consideration.

A jockey must be named at the time of entry by the trainer. A jockey that is engaged to ride a horse is bound to fulfill his/her engagement unless he/she is excused by the stewards. If a rider becomes injured or ill enroute to the starting gate, the stewards will designate a substitute rider, and that rider will fulfill the order of the stewards and complete the engagement on the horse.

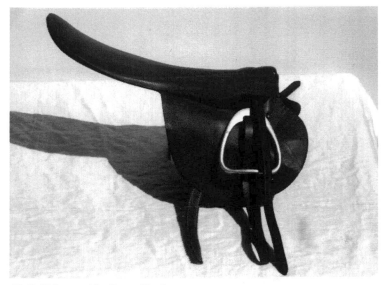

10-8. Riding saddle (Gerry Mora)

The race goer should never overlook a sudden switch of jockeys in a particular race. A sudden switch in riders will usually occur on the day of the race or just minutes before post. The sudden switch in jockeys is announced to the betting public as soon as possible via the public address system at the racetrack. The following are some reasons for a sudden switch in jockeys:

The assigned jockey fell ill just prior to the race.

The assigned jockey failed to make the assigned weight.

The assigned jockey was involved in a riding accident in a prior race and is physically unable to ride.

The assigned jockey failed to report to the jockey's room for some reason.

Sometimes jockeys will switch from one horse that they rode successfully in the past to a different horse in the current race. You should ask yourself why. Unlike the sudden switch, the following are reasons for a jockey to switch horses entered in the same race:

The horse that did well for the jockey last time out does not fit the conditions as well in the current race.

The new horse is part of a large stable, and the jockey is looking at future engagements with a particular trainer.

Before a jockey is able to get on good horses in a stable, he or she is forced to accept other mounts from the trainer that may not have much of a chance of winning.

The jockey's agent has committed his/her client to ride a different horse due to a prior agreement with a trainer.

Some of the best handicappers in the business of horseracing are jockey agents. Their function is to secure mounts for their jockey clients. The agent is hired by the individual jockey for this task.

A good jockey agent is familiar with all the trainers on the racetrack grounds as well as their horses. Agents must determine which horses present the best chances for their jockey clients to win. For obtaining riding commitments for their clients, agents receive a percentage (usually 20% to 30%) of their jockey's earnings. Jockey agents must have a thorough knowledge of the horseracing industry, and they must have the ability to handicap a race in order to determine which horse will have the best chance to win.

It would be wise for the race goer to review the jockey standings, which are published daily in the racing newspapers and programs. The jockey standings are merely an indication of how a jockey is currently doing against fellow riders at a particular racetrack. The jockey standings are very similar in format to that of the trainers' standings. The racing program and *The Daily Racing Form* will list the jockey standings at a current race meet according to the number of mounts; the number of wins, seconds, and thirds; and the winning percentage (the number of wins to the number of mounts).

This will enable you to determine which jockeys are getting the most from their mounts. Not all jockeys, as good as they may be, fit every horse. On the other hand, you will find horses that will respond equally well to any rider that is placed on their backs. Of course there are those horses that can never win no matter who rides them. A good jockey is one that is able to save some of his/her mount's vital energy for the final portion of the race. They are able to break their mounts alertly from the starting gate and remain calm and patient while awaiting the opportunity to make a move during the race and finish strong. There are many factors that are part of the makeup of a good jockey; for instance, good hands (meaning the ability to determine through the feel of the reins how much horse is under him/her) or expert use of the whip at the precise time with the ability to switch hands quickly and smoothly. For all practical purposes, the major traits of a good jockey are the following:

INTELLIGENCE: The jockey must be able to make split-second decisions during the running of a race as well as be able to evaluate the competition.

COURAGE: The good rider is one who is able to keep calm behind other horses during the race, and when a small opening appears, to go for it. The poor rider will hesitate and go around horses, losing precious lengths that may well cost the race.

A SENSE OF PACE: This trait comes with experience. The more horses a jockey rides, the more he or she realizes how fast the horse is running and how fast a race is going.

X-FACTOR: Finally, there is an unknown factor, which can be best described as an unexplainable ability to make a horse run better than it normally does. It seems to be an ability to communicate with the horse in a special way to obtain the maximum effort capable of the horse.

A poor jockey is one who exhausts his or her mount by constantly applying restraint throughout the race in order to slow the horse down when in fact it would be better to allow the horse to run and relax on its own. These riders will get their mounts up to top speed after leaving the gate and create a huge lead over the other horses and wind up in the back of the field at the finish. A good horse with a good jockey stands a better chance to win a race than a good horse with a poor jockey.

Now that you have a basic understanding of the sport of horseracing, you can now apply that knowledge to your wagering decisions.

HANDICAPPING AND WAGERING

In addition to the excitement of watching horseracing, most track visitors decide to place a bet on the outcome of a race. A small wager adds enjoyment to the experience and can be rewarding both figuratively and literally if one picks a winner. Many people simply place bets on a particular horse because of its name, the color of its silks, or the fact that it has the highest odds to win a race. But if you make some simple observations before placing a bet, not only will you increase your enjoyment and appreciation of the sport, there is a higher probability that you will pick that elusive winner.

Handicapping

Handicapping is the process by which the bettor attempts to select the horse with the best chance to win a race on the basis of past performances.

Before any wager is made on a horse race, one must be able to apply sound handicapping principals in order to be successful at the races. Most racing fans know little or nothing about the art of handicapping horses. There is no greater thrill than the ability to select your own winners in a race. Selecting winners in horseracing is similar to making successful investments in the stock market. Actually, the serious handicapper has more relevant data at his or her command to predict the outcome of a race than the stockbroker has to predict what a particular stock will do on the market.

The element of luck and chance sometimes upsets the best and most careful calculations. The reader must understand that in order to become a successful handicapper, one must utilize the proper tools. The tools required to properly handicap a horse race include a general knowledge of the sport and the past performance charts found in *The Daily Racing Form* and other racing publications. It goes without saying that *The Daily Racing Form* is, to all serious handicappers, as important as the *Wall Street Journal* is to the stock investor. Without *The Daily Racing Form*, no horseplayer can ever hope to be a successful handicapper at the racetrack. It is important for the bettor to learn how to read the past performance charts of a horse as they appear in *The Daily Racing Form* and racing programs. For assistance in accomplishing this task, please refer to Appendix C (How to Read *The Daily Racing Form*). You won't win at the racetrack if you don't do your homework. Whatever your reasons for selecting and reading this book, you will certainly come away not only with a solid understanding of horseracing as a sport but an improved ability to select the best horse in any given race.

HANDICAPPING PROCESS

The basic handicapping process consists of considering the major factors: date of last race, distance, class, weight, speed, track condition, trainer, jockey, and post position. These factors are all part of the overall handicapping process and should be considered as a group and not on an individual basis. Let us now discuss these factors in greater detail. The handicapping hints listed under each factor are designed to assist the bettor in selecting the horse with the best possible chance of winning.

DATE OF LAST RACE: It is inadvisable to place a wager on a horse that hasn't raced recently. A recent race is usually considered to be within 30 days of the current race. There is good reason to believe that a horse may have developed a physical infirmity if it has not raced within a 30-day period. However, there are some horses that seem to run better when they have been away, or are fresh. A horse may be away from the races for several months and then come back with a good performance in its first race back. Before you wager on such a horse, be sure that the trainer is able to demonstrate through his/her past performances the ability and skill to get a winning effort from a horse after a long layoff from the races. The horse's past performances must also demonstrate its ability to win after a layoff of more than 30 days.

The date of the last race will vary with the type of race. It has long been known that 70% of all cheaper claiming race sprint runners have raced within a 14-day period prior to their winning race. It is also a known fact that better-quality allowance, handicap, and stakes horses are capable of holding their peak condition for a longer period of time than their cheaper counterparts. It is not unusual to see a hard-running claiming horse race as often as 25 times or more in one year. Similarly, it is noted that most of the top stakes and handicap horses will only race 7 to 10 times within the same period.

Hint: In claiming sprint races, preference should be given to those horses that have raced within the last 30 days.

DISTANCE: Of course, virtually any racehorse can run any distance—the question is, naturally, how fast can it perform this task? Most racehorses are either sprinters or routers. Carefully review the past performances of all the entries in a race and eliminate any horses that are entered at an improper distance for them. If a horse has a record of only running in 6-furlong sprints and it is entered in a current race at a mile and a quarter distance, it would be best to eliminate this horse as a possible wager. Horses that perform poorly at both sprint and route races are probably still seeking a racing distance that best suits their talent. Only select those horses that have demonstrated through past performance charts their ability to run well at the current distance.

Hint: The past performances will indicate whether a horse prefers sprints or distance events. Sprinters rarely run well when asked to race more than a mile. Routers are at a disadvantage when asked to race less than a mile. In races of a mile or longer, there is time to overcome a poor start.

CLASS: Determining the true class of a racehorse is extremely important and perhaps the most difficult task in handicapping a race. Class is speed and the courage and ability to sustain it over a distance of ground. Racehorses with superior class will easily defeat inferior-class horses because they have greater speed. A horse with class can take the lead in a race and remain there, they are able to come from behind other horses, and they are capable of producing tremendous bursts of speed at any stage of a race. It is this ability to turn on high speed when needed that makes for a difference in class among racehorses. The class horse is also able to overcome weight, poor track conditions, poor post position, and all other obstacles that it may encounter during the running of a race.

The type of race in which a horse competes is considered by most professional handicappers to be an excellent indicator of a horse's class level. Horses running in claiming races are considered to be the lowest grade of Thoroughbreds. Claiming races are for the least expensive, ordinary, and slower racehorses. Claiming races are the most frequently scheduled races offered at racetracks. On a normal racing day in which 9 races are offered to the betting public, 5 to 6 races will be for a specific claiming price. The claiming race is an excellent race for the bettor to handicap. The reason for this is that the value of the claiming race indicates the true class or level of competition for each horse entered. A $15,000.00 claiming race will usually draw entries whose value will be appraised by their owners or trainers to be $15,000.00. It is easy to see that a horse competing and losing at the $8,000.00 claiming level would not have much of a chance of winning if entered and running against $15,000.00 claiming horses. Each claiming race will offer a purse for the owners of the entries. For example, a $25,000.00 claiming race will have a purse value of $16,000.00. A further detailed explanation of a claiming race is presented in chapter 12.

Allowance races usually feature unsuccessful stakes and handicap horses as well as horses that have graduated from the claiming ranks. In handicap races, we find stake horses stepping down in class and allowance horses stepping up in class. Finally, the highest plateau in horseracing is the stakes race. In the stakes race, the best-quality horses compete for the highest purses. In horseracing, the higher the class of horse, the more consistent is its performance. It is important for the bettor to evaluate the true class or value of each horse in a race to determine if the horse belongs in the same company as the other horses in the same race. The class of an individual can only be accomplished by evaluating and examining a horse's complete past performance chart. The past performance charts will indicate at what point(s) during a race the horse exhibited speed. It will also indicate the types and values of past races for each horse.

Hint: Sharp drops in claiming price ($5,000.00 or more) usually suggest that there is something wrong with the horse. Maidens are considered to be running over their head when they are entered against winners. It is better to select a horse that is improving and moving up the claiming ranks than a horse with poor form that is dropping down in class. Maiden races with first-time starters are difficult to handicap due to the lack of any past performances. It's best to pass and not wager on these types of races. The cheaper the horse, the less consistent its performance. Do not assume that a horse has class if it has a handicap or stakes race in its past performance.

WEIGHT: "Weight will stop a freight train" is an old saying used around the racetrack. The amount of weight carried by a racehorse in a race is one of the most important factors in the handicapping process. In most races, horses are assigned different weights to make the race a more even proposition. This is particularly true in handicap races in which the racing secretary attempts to assign more weight to the more mature and faster horses and less weight to the younger or less productive horses. The theoretical goal of these weight assignments by the racing secretary is to bring all the horses in the race to the finish line at the same time. Most weight is expressed through the jockey and his/her equipment. Additional weight is in the form of lead bars placed in pockets of a pad that is placed under the racing saddle. If a horse is scheduled to carry 118 pounds in a race and the jockey with equipment weighs only 114 pounds, then 4 pounds of lead weight must be added to the weight assignment. Sometimes the extra pounds assigned simply are not enough, and top-weighted horses win much more often than low-weighted horses. This is especially true in sprint races than route races. This simply means that the farther the distance a horse has to race, the more weight becomes a factor.

Hint: The past performances will indicate if a horse is at a disadvantage when carrying a high weight (120 pounds or more). The weight factor is more meaningful in distance races than in sprint races. In distance races, any weight change of 5 pounds or more since the last race should be regarded as significant. Top-weighted horses are usually considered to be the best horses based on their past performance or by the opinion of the racing secretary.

SPEED: If it were possible to select the one single determining factor in winning races, it would have to be speed. When you are betting on the horses, you must consider the rate of speed. Speed is not only a good estimate of a horse's ability but it is also an important factor for consideration as part of the handicapping process. This is the reason why speed ratings appear in racing publications. The speed ratings appearing in *The Daily Racing Form* are based on the best times recorded during the past 3 years. A horse earns a speed rating of 100 by equaling the time for the distance, and 1 point is deducted for each 1/5 of a second slower than the standard. The standard speed rating for each horse is printed on the horse's past performance chart. Another important factor for consideration in the area of speed are the Beyer speed figures.

The Beyer speed figures are another handicapping tool available to the bettor. These figures allow the bettor to evaluate every performance in the career of each horse entered in a race. The Beyer speed figures are printed in the past performance charts of *The Daily Racing Form*. They were created by Andrew Beyer, a popular Thoroughbred handicapper and racing columnist for over 20 years. He is the author of the book *Picking Winners*, which was first published in 1975 and was based on speed figures. Basically, the Beyer speed figures make it easy for the bettor to make comparisons of individual horses between different distances and racetracks. They are merely numerical representations of a horse's past performance, based on the final time of the race and the speed over the racetrack in which the race was contested. The higher the Beyer speed figure, the better the performance. Some of the best horses in the country will earn a Beyer speed figure of 115+, while horses competing at the bottom-level, $2,500.00

claiming races at small racetracks may earn a 57 Beyer speed figure. Smarty Jones received a 118 Beyers speed figure as a 3 year old. This 118 figure represents the highest Beyer speed figure ever given to a 3-year-old Thoroughbred.

Speed figures are an excellent beginning for any novice or professional handicapper, but they should be regarded as a starting point to the application of all the other handicapping factors.

Hint: Be aware of the horse that experienced a nose-to-nose stretch drive in its last race, the effort likely took a lot out of it. If there are several speed horses in a race, be aware of those horses that come from behind, especially in distance races. A horse that illustrates improvement in breaking alertly from the starting gate is telling you that it is ready.

TRACK CONDITION: On an off or muddy racetrack, the bettor must consider that the selections for a fast/dry track will not run to expectations. Due to poor track conditions, some may be scratched from the race by the trainer and may not run at all. It is important for the bettor to take note if the horse is wearing shoes with mud calks to ensure its ability to handle an off or muddy track. Consult the shoe board in the paddock area or listen carefully to the public announcements regarding any changes in the race. The best way to determine how a horse will perform over any given track surface is to review the Tomlinson ratings found in the career box of the past performance chart of *The Daily Racing Form*. Refer to chapter 7 for a complete description of the Tomlinson ratings.

Hint: Select frontrunners whenever the track is sloppy or muddy. A horse with a proven mud record through its past performances is preferred over horses that have not raced well when the track is off. A horse with a proven turf record gets the nod over horses that have run poorly on the turf as well as those that have never raced on the turf. On muddy racetracks, the inside post position will draw the water drainage, making it slower going.

TRAINER: The Thoroughbred racehorse is a fragile creature, and it requires a great deal of skill and patience on the part of the trainer to keep it in competition. A horse that is stretching out in distance or stepping up in class may not be able to handle the task if the trainer is incompetent. If a horse has recently changed trainers, it would be wise for the bettor to take note of the new trainer's winning percentage as it compares to that of the old trainer. If the new trainer has a higher winning percentage, then the horse's chances of winning are good. Winning percentages are easily found in the trainers' standings in *The Daily Racing Form* or the racing program. The successful bettor should be able to detect through the past performance charts the various training patterns of a trainer including their strengths and weaknesses. Some of these patterns would include their ability to win races with horses after a long layoff period, first-time starters, turf runners, newly claimed horses, horses stepping up in class, etc. It should become clear to the bettor that a horse that exhibits a good recent winning form, trained by a successful trainer, is considered to be an excellent wager.

Hint: Trainers do make judgment errors when training their horses, and if you are alert, you will be able to separate the competent from the incompetent. The trainer knows more about his/her horse than anyone else. The competing trainers are next in line as to the knowledge about a particular horse.

JOCKEY: The role of the jockey in the handicapping process is an important consideration. If you expect to win at the races, you can't wager on the jockey alone and disregard the ability of the horse. It is absolutely essential to have the right jockey to ensure the safety of your wager. It would be in the bettor's best interest to determine the winning percentage of each jockey in the race. This is accomplished by consulting the local jockey standings appearing in *The Daily Racing Form* and racing program. The names of the good jockeys will usually appear in the top 5 of the standings. A top jockey can accurately estimate the speed of the pace and estimate the amount of energy his/her horse has left to finish strongly. A pace-conscious jockey and a fit horse is an ideal combination to winning races.

Hint: Jockeys riding in good form attract good mounts. Bet the horse, not the jockey. Be aware of a change from a poor rider to a good rider; the horse should be considered. Horses ridden by the highest-rated jockeys usually draw lower odds than they deserve.

POST POSITION: Post position can certainly make a difference in either victory or defeat, especially when the starting gate is placed close to a turn in a distance race. In this instance, horses located in the outside post positions (6 through 12) are likely to give up valuable ground in the early running and finish a couple lengths behind where they would have finished with a ground-saving inside post. Horses in a 6-furlong sprint race on the average 1-mile racetrack have a long run to the first turn. With a long run to the first turn, most horses and riders have plenty of time to secure a normal running position up front or just off the pace. Post position is considered by most professional handicappers to be a more important factor in distance races than in sprint races. The bettor should examine the past performances to determine a horse's racing ability from the different post positions. For instance, a horse may show a winning pattern from inside post positions only.

Hint: When all other things are equal, the horse with the inside post position has less ground to cover than the horse with an outside post. The inside post is not an advantage unless the horse has early speed.

MISCELLANEOUS HANDICAPPING HINTS: Fillies and mares (females) are better suited to a race against members of their own sex. They are at a definite disadvantage when asked to run against colts and geldings (males). As a rule, in races for Thoroughbreds of different ages, the older animals have the advantage. A horse that has had race experience over a particular racetrack is a better bet than one who has shipped in from another track. A sleek-looking horse is usually a healthy horse. A horse should have a published timed workout within the past 10 days. All selections should be made only after all scratches have been announced. A horse in good form will exhibit at least 2 in-the-money efforts in its last 3 races. It is not necessary to wager on every race. Most importantly, never wager more money than you can afford to lose.

Selecting winners and acquiring knowledge about the sport of horseracing can certainly add to your enjoyment and insight. But none of this can replace the satisfaction that comes from increasing your profits and reducing your losses at the racetrack. Your ultimate objective as a bettor is to win—to beat the horses instead of allowing them to beat you. Remember that pari-mutuel wagering is a battle of wits and self-discipline between yourself and the mass of horseplayers at the racetrack.

Wagering

Wagering at the racetrack is merely the bettor's means of financially backing a selected horse to win a race. If the backed horse wins, the bettor is rewarded with a monetary profit over and above the initial wager. Pari-mutuel wagering was the invention of Pierre Oller, a perfume shop owner in Paris, France, in 1865. Mr. Oller would sell tickets on the races and keep the monies collected in one common pool. He would deduct a 5% handling fee and distribute the remainder of the pool to the winners. He called this system *perier mutuel,* meaning "mutual stake," or "wagering among ourselves." As this betting method became popular in England, it was called Paris mutuals, and later became known as parimutuels.

In 1933, the first Totalisator machine in the United States was installed at Arlington Park outside of Chicago by the American Totalisator Company. All monies wagered before a race are pooled in a separate win pool, a place (second-place) pool, and a show (third-place) pool. The odds for each horse are set by the odds maker, who is an individual employed by the racetrack. The duty of the odds maker is to set the odds based on past performances of each horse entered in each race on any given day. The odds are printed in the racing program as well as the daily racing publications. These early odds are referred to as the morning line. As money wagered begins to accumulate before each race, the totalisator machine adds the various amounts wagered and computes the odds that the bettors establish on each horse. These odds are then flashed onto the tote board located in the infield facing the grandstand (Figure 11-1).

Wagering on the races on site begins early in the day when the racetrack officially opens for business. A bettor is able to wager on any race during the day simply by telling the mutual clerk the specific race in which he or she wishes to place a wager. Bettors are able to do the same through off-track betting parlors or through telephone wagering accounts.

The odds for each separate pool are determined by the amount of money wagered on each horse by the betting public. The odds and amounts wagered in each pool change approximately every 60 seconds. These changes are brought about by the wagers made by the betting public. These changes are automatically relayed to the infield tote board by the totalisator machine located in a central control room before each race. All wagering ceases when the first horse

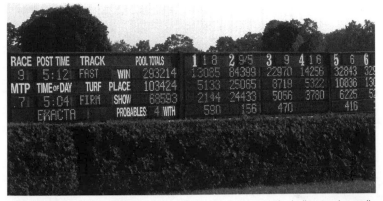

11-1. The tote board registers information about a race, including track conditions, odds, and number and pole position of each horse. (Joel Silva)

enters the starting gate. The odds that appear on the tote board at that time are final.

If a horse closes at 5 to 1 odds to win, it means that the bettor will receive $10.00 in return for every $2.00 wagered, plus the $2.00 initially wagered, for a total return of $12.00.

The race goer should be familiar with the various types of wagers available at the racetrack. The two groups of wagers offered by most racetracks are basic wagers and exotic wagers.

BASIC WAGERS

Basic wagers consist of win, place, show, across the board, and daily double.

WIN: The horse must win the race in order for the bettor to cash a win ticket.

PLACE: The horse must finish either first or second for the bettor to cash a place ticket. The place payoff is usually less than half of the win payoff.

SHOW: The horse must finish first, second, or third for a bettor to cash a show ticket. Show wagering is usually omitted by most racetracks when there are only 4 horses in a race.

The show payoff is almost always less than a third of the win payoff.

ACROSS THE BOARD: Sometimes referred to as a combination wager. A bet placed on a horse to win, place, and show. This means betting $2.00 to win, $2.00 to place, and $2.00 to show on one ticket at a total cost of $6.00. Naturally, amounts higher than $2.00 may be wagered.

DAILY DOUBLE: In this type of wager, the bettor must select the winners of 2 races, usually the first and second race of the program. All monies wagered on the daily double are placed in a separate pool. It is considered a risky wager due to the fact that it is very difficult to select 2 winners in succession. You must place your wager prior to the first race without physically inspecting the horses in the second race—this is a definite disadvantage to the bettor in the handicapping process.

EXOTIC WAGERS

The various types of exotic wagers include perfecta or exacta, quinella, triple or trifecta, superfecta, pick 3 or 4, and pick 6.

PERFECTA OR EXACTA: The perfecta and exacta are essentially the same type of wager. The bettor must select 2 horses in a single race—1 to finish first and a second horse to finish second, in that exact order. The perfect 1-2 selection is required to win. All the monies wagered for this type of wager are entered into a separate betting pool.

QUINELLA: This is a separate wagering pool in which the bettor must select 2 horses in the same race to finish either first or second. If either horse selected wins and the other selected horse finishes second, the bettor will receive a winning payoff. A 1-2 or 2-1 finish results in a winning ticket. A winning quinella ticket will result in a lower payoff than a winning perfecta or exacta payoff.

Triple or trifecta: This type of wager may be offered in any of the races on a daily program. All monies wagered on a triple or trifecta race are entered into a separate wagering pool. The bettor is required to select the first 3 finishers in a single race in their exact order of finish. It is a very popular type of wager due to its high-valued payoffs.

Superfecta: This type of exotic wager is usually reserved for the final race of the day. The superfecta wager covers a single combination of 4 horses, which must finish in the exact order that was specified when the betting ticket was purchased. Superfecta tickets may sell at $2.00 or $3.00 apiece, depending on the racetrack. A separate wagering pool is required for all superfecta wagers. A high-valued payoff is normal for this type of wager.

Pick 3 or 4: This type of wager requires the bettor to select either 3 or 4 winners in 3 or 4 separate specified races on the program. It is a difficult task for most bettors, but the financial rewards are high. All monies wagered on the pick 3 or 4 are placed in a separate wagering pool. The ticket must be purchased before the first of the 3 or 4 races to be run. There is usually a mandatory payout daily of the entire wagering pool.

Pick 6: This is a more difficult wager than the pick 3 or 4. In this case, the bettor is required to pick 6 consecutive winners in order to cash in on a high payoff. Naturally, the ticket must be purchased before the first of the 6 designated races is run. If there are no winners on any given day, 75% of the money in the required separate wagering pool is then carried over to the next racing day. Therefore, it is easy to see how a pick 6 payoff can be very lucrative. On the other hand, if there are 3 winners of the pick 6 pool, the payoff is then divided equally with the 3 winners. A consolation payoff is always awarded daily to those bettors who selected 5 of the 6 winners.

In the pick 3 or 4 and the pick 6 wagering, if there is a late scratch, the bettor automatically receives the actual betting favorite in the race.

Most bettors who wager on exotic types of wagers will combine or box their wagers in order to increase their chances of winning. By boxing their wagers, they are covering all possible combinations of their selections. The more selections in a boxed wager, the higher the cost of the ticket. For example, a $2.00 exacta box for 2 horses will cost a total of $4.00, and a similar wager on a 6-horse box will result in a total cost of $60.00.

The race goer should become familiar with other wagering situations that may occur while visiting a racetrack. One must know when a race becomes official. After each race the infield tote board will display the word "official" to relay to the betting public that the race is official and that there are no claims of foul reported. Once a race is declared official, the payoff prices are displayed. Never discard your betting tickets before a race is declared official. If the word "inquiry" is displayed after the running of a race, it means that the stewards are investigating the running of the race or a particular jockey. If the word "objection" is displayed after the race, it means that the jockey, trainer, or owner has lodged an official claim of foul. Based on the outcome of an investigation, there is always the possibility that the order of finish may be changed. If any of the first 4 finishers are involved in the investigation, their numbers will flash on the tote board until the race becomes official.

Another wagering situation confronting the bettor is the overlay. This phenomenon occurs when a horse exhibits an excellent chance of winning based on its outstanding racing record, but the present high odds do not reflect the horse's true winning ability. Basically, it means that the betting public may have overlooked this horse as a betting favorite.

APPROXIMATE TRACK PAYOFF
TO WIN ($2.00)
IF THE ODDS ARE

ODDS	PAYS	ODDS	PAYS
1-5	2.40	8-5	5.20
2-5	2.80	9-5	5.60
1-2	3.00	2	6.00
3-5	3.20	5-2	7.00
4-5	3.60	3	8.00
Even	4.00	7-2	9.00
6-5	4.40	4	10.00
7-5	4.80	9-2	11.00
3-2	5.00	5	12.00

11-2. Payoff for a $2.00 wager. (Author)

Another situation involving wagering is when a bettor may choose to parlay all winning bets. In order to parlay a bet, the bettor takes all the proceeds from a winning bet and wagers it on another bet. The race goer should also be aware of multiple entries in a race called an entry on the program. An entry is when 2 or more horses in the same race have the same owner. Both horses are listed in the program as a single betting entity. Now the bettor is getting 2 or 3 horses to bet, at the cost of betting on 1 horse in a race. When a bettor places a wager on an entry, the wager is automatically placed on all the horses listed as part of the entry.

When visiting a racetrack, one might hear the term "chalk horse." This term refers to the betting favorite of the race. The opposite of a chalk horse is a long shot, which refers to any horse in a race with odds at 10 to 1 or higher.

For assistance in determining the approximate payoffs at various odds on a $2.00 wager, refer to Figure 11-2. All wagering and payoffs are performed at any of the mutual windows where a mutual clerk will assist you in placing your wager. In order to place any wager at the racetrack, one must

Thunder Downs

2   One Mile

Claiming
Purse $ 5,000 . For fillies and mares Three years old and upward.
May 20, 2004. Three year olds 122lbs.; Older 124 lbs. Claiming price $4,000.

	T. Owner	T. Trainer	3 - 1
1	Green with yellow 'O', Yellow Sleeves.		
	Star	$ 4,000	J. Jockey
⇒ (p.p. 4)	B.m. 6 Cloud S. - Twinkle	124	

	T. Owner	T. Trainer	3 - 1
1a	Green with yellow 'O', Yellow Sleeves		
	Blaze	$ 4,000	K. Jockey
⇒ (p.p. 6)	Ch. m. 4 Fire - Kindling	124	

11-3. Racing program indicating the horse's number and post position. (Author)

state the race number of the wager, state the amount of the wager, state the type of wager, and state the program number of the horse(s).

A horse's program number and saddlecloth number are one and the same, however, the actual post position may differ from the program number. For example, a horse may appear as number 1 in the program, but its actual post position in the starting gate is number 5. This usually occurs in those races in which there is an entry of more than one horse by a trainer. The post position is listed just below the program number in parentheses; for example, (p.p. 5) (Figure 11-3).

Another point to consider when viewing the program is the appearance of letters within parentheses after a horse's name. These letters indicate that the horse was born and bred in a foreign country. An asterisk was used in front of a horse's name up until 1977 for the same purpose. It is important for the bettor to realize that horses from foreign countries primarily race on turf at distances of a mile or more. This information may prove valuable when attempting to handicap a turf race run at a distance in the United States. Examples of notations of a foreign birth are Ireland (IRE), Brazil (BRZ), Great Britain (GB), and France (FR).

Off-Track Betting (OTB)

The topic of wagering on the outcome of a horse race can not be complete unless off-track betting is mentioned. Off-track betting, more commonly known as OTB, refers to legalized betting conducted away from the racetrack where the horse race is actually being run. It is usually operated and supervised by individual racetracks or state and local authorities.

In 1946, American wagering on horseracing was at its peak, with New York State being the one exception to this trend. At the time, New York City's Mayor O'Dwyer imposed a 0.05% tax on all wagering. The "O'Dwyer bite," as it was named, was considered by many to be the precursor of modern day off-track betting. Just as it was then, it is now considered to be an easy source of tax revenue for city, county, and state treasuries. Although legal (off-track wagering existed for many years in other countries), it is comparatively recent in this country. In 1971, New York became the first state to operate pari-mutuel wagering away from the track. However, these OTB betting parlors were not owned or operated by the racing association but rather by the City of New York. It wasn't long before other regions and counties within the state got aboard the bandwagon. These OTB operators merely had to pay the racing association a small percentage on all wagering while they reaped in large profits for their treasuries.

Today OTB parlors exist throughout the country. With the introduction of simulcasting via satellite transmission, it is now possible to wager on races at racetracks located in other states and other countries on any given day. OTB parlors owned and operated by local and state municipalities have had a definite effect on the overall reduction of racetrack attendance. These OTB parlors provide a convenient means for the bettor to legally place a wager without actually going to the racetrack. However, on-track payoffs are higher than those at the OTB parlor. For example, if a horse wins a race and pays $52.00 to win at the track, it may only pay out $49.40 to those bettors holding a winning ticket at an OTB parlor. This is due to a 0.05% surcharge imposed by the OTB corporation on each wager. Needless to say, these OTB parlors owned and operated by municipalities have had a negative effect on horseracing. As daily racetrack attendance declines, the revenue generated through on-track wagering also declines, which in turn affects the amount of purse money distributed to the horse people. If purses decline, then horsemen and women migrate to other racing jurisdictions offering a better purse structure. The community surrounding the racetrack then also suffers financially with the loss of business, jobs, and tax revenue if the horse people leave or the racetrack is closed.

Learning from the negative experience of the New York OTB system in the 1970's, many racetracks now operate their own OTB parlors and pay on-track prices to their patrons.

Over the years, legalized gambling has certainly taken its toll on the horseracing industry. Today, with state lotteries and casino gambling, horseracing has gone from the only game in town to simply another venue competing for the leisure dollar of the gambler.

Racetracks are now fighting back by operating their own gambling casinos on their premises. All the money that is generated through gaming is directly returned to the racetrack operation and purse structure for the horsemen and women. Racetracks throughout the country that were on the verge of collapse and bankruptcy are now flourishing financially.

Touts

At this point, the reader should be aware of the scam artists called "touts" that plague the racetracks. A tout is a person attending the races who will approach unaware bettors in order to swindle them out of their money by letting them in on a so-called sure winner. Most states have laws against touting, but very rarely are they enforced. The goal of the tout is to have a gullible bettor give him or her money for a tip as well as placing a free wager on a horse for this inside information. Naturally if the tip is successful, the bettor will feel compelled to reward the tout financially.

The process of touting is very simple. The tout will select a race with about 8 entries where there is no outstanding favorite. He then approaches 8 different people at the track and gives each of them the name of one of the 8 entries. The tout will identify each of his targets by writing on his program the bettor's name or some distinguishing notation next to each entry's number. For example, if the tout approaches a woman in a yellow dress and tells her to bet number 4 to win, he would then write "yellow dress" on his program next to horse number 4.

Since he has now touted every horse in the race, one of the 8 bettors he approached will be a winner. That person is usually ecstatic to be a winner. The bettor now feels at last, they have a bona-fide connection who they can count on for the real inside dope. At this point, the tout will cash in on the bettor's enthusiasm. After the race, the tout will reunite with his one winner, and after receiving the financial reward, the tout will tell the winner that he/she has an even better prospect in another race but that additional money will be needed in order to place a large bet. Many bettors will fall for the tout's line and agree to pay a larger fee or place a bet. The touting process then starts all over again.

The tout may even cash in on the second-place horse in the same race. Many of the gullible bettors are excited even if their horse finishes second. The second-place horse may have been a long shot and paid a large payoff for a place and show wager. The tout will approach the target bettor after the race and complain about how the horse got bumped or stumbled at the start or some other lame excuse for why the horse failed to win. The tout then promises the bettor a better outcome next time. It is amazing to see the number of bettors that will look to the tout time and time again for more supposedly inside information. It is better to do your own handicapping and not rely on such information. The best advice that can be given to the reader is that there is no such thing as a sure thing.

Money Management

Knowing what horse to place a wager is not the only requirement for success at the racetrack. The other requirement is knowing how to wager. Being a successful handicapper is one thing; knowing how to manage your money is another. Proper money management requires a high degree of discipline. Bettors must always be in full control of their emotions and not overreact to either victory or defeat. Managing your money and emotions are skills easily developed. It simply takes time, patience, and determination. The average racing fan has very poor money-management skills. After a few losing wagers, panic sets in, all wagers thereafter become too large, and selections are made with poor judgment, making for a very unenjoyable and frustrating day at the races. A wise bettor must concentrate on keeping losses at a minimum. You must decide before going to the racetrack just how much money you can afford to lose, then discipline yourself not to exceed that figure. With a loss limit in place, you can now place your wagers with good judgment and with confidence.

TYPES OF RACES

Many racing fans do not fully comprehend the important differences in the various types of races offered each day at a racetrack. This chapter will provide the reader with a clear understanding of types of races offered daily. There are 4 basic classifications of races that are offered for wagering to the public on a daily basis (Figure 12-1). In ascending order of quality, they are claiming races, allowance races, handicap races, and stake races.

CLAIMING RACE: This type of race is one in which all horses entered may be claimed (purchased) at a previously established claiming price. The claiming price may be as low as $1,000.00 and as high as $100,000.00, depending on the racetrack. Most racetracks restrict claiming to those owners who have horses already stabled on the premises. Claiming races are for the least expensive and most erratic Thoroughbreds and are the most frequently scheduled races. On average, there are twice as many claiming races as there are allowance races and 4 times as many claiming races as there are stake and handicap races. The reason for these ratios is simple. In the world of Thoroughbred racing, outstanding individuals like Man O' War, Secretariat, Smarty Jones, Kelso, and Seabiscuit are few and far between. For every super horse, there are hundreds and hundreds of physically able but essentially ordinary horses. The claiming race

12-1 Pyramid of types of racing in ascending order of quality. (Author)

provides the owners of horses with minimal talent an opportunity to win purses and at the same time offers numerous wagering opportunities to the betting public. If a trainer or owner wishes to claim a horse out of a claiming race, he or she must submit a claim form and put it into the claiming box before the start of the race. Once the race is over, the box is opened and ownership is transferred. If there is more than one claim for the same horse, then the new owner is decided by lot. In the case of multiple claims for the same horse, the stewards or racing secretary will conduct what is called a shake to determine the new owner.

This process involves the use of a bottle with numbered balls. If there are 3 claims on the same horse, then 3 numbered balls are placed in the bottle. Each claim slip is numbered on the back so that it is identified with the number appearing on the ball. The steward or racing secretary will shake the bottle with the 3 balls inside and shake out one of the balls from the bottle. The winner of the shake is determined to be the new owner. When the field of claimers are released from the starting gate, a claimed horse becomes the property of the new owner. Ownership is transferred to the new owner after the race even if the horse becomes injured or has to be destroyed. If the claimed horse happens to earn any of the purse money in the race, it is automatically transferred to the former owner. The money representing the claiming price is also transferred to the former owner. The rules of racing at most racetracks specify that for a 30-day period after claiming a horse, the new owner is required to enter the horse to race for a claiming price 25% higher or keep the horse idle. If a horse is claimed for $10,000.00, the new owner must race the horse back for at least $12,500.00 or wait till the 30-day period has expired. After the horse has raced for $12,500.00, the new owner may enter the horse at any claiming price desired. This 30-day waiting period is usually referred to as "being in jail" for a recently claimed horse. It should be understood that for each race offered to the betting public, claiming or otherwise, there is always a monetary purse available for the owners of the horses. A $50,000.00 claiming race may have a purse value of $35,000.00.

An owner of a horse entered in a $50,000.00 claiming race can safely assume that the other horses in the race are also of a $50,000.00 value, or thereabouts. Consequently, the owner has an excellent chance to win a purse valued at $35,000.00. An owner of a Thoroughbred that has been successfully campaigning at a $50,000.00 claiming level might decide to enter his horse in a $35,000.00 claiming race so that he can walk away with a $20,000.00 purse. This certainly sounds like a good idea, but the probability that his $50,000.00 horse may be claimed for $35,000.00 by another owner promptly causes him to reconsider his decision. As far as the bettor is concerned, if the owners in a claiming race have, by and large, equal chances at the purse, then the bettor can be sure that the ability and talent of the horses in the race are evenly matched.

ALLOWANCE RACE: The next higher grade of races offered to the betting public is the allowance race. Horses entered into an allowance race cannot be claimed. It is the type of race in which the weights carried by each horse are dictated by the conditions of the race as determined by the racing secretary. The conditions of the race determine whether a horse will carry more or less weight based on the age of the horse, the number of wins, amount of money won, and the type of races it has won. Other conditions for an allowance race might include stipulations such as being nonwinners of 2 races or 3 year olds that have not won $10,000.00 since January 5. Weight allowances are distributed in order to penalize horses that have a winning record with a heavier weight assignment and to give a lighter weight assignment to those horses that have a poor racing record.

A horse that has won 3 races within a month may be assigned to carry 6 pounds more than a nonwinner during the same time period. Allowance races will usually draw entries consisting of unsuccessful stake and handicap horses whose owners and trainers are searching for a winning spot for them as well as horses who have distinguished themselves within the claiming ranks.

HANDICAP RACE: This is a type of race in which the racing secretary assigns weights to the horses in order to equalize their chances of winning. In the handicap race, the racing secretary determines the weight to be carried by each horse based on his/her evaluation of a horse's racing ability. Therefore, the difference between a handicap race and an allowance race is that in a handicap race, the racing secretary determines the weight assignment; and in an allowance race, the conditions of the race determine the weight assignments. The goal of the racing secretary in assigning weight in a handicap race is to theoretically have all the horses in a race reach the finish line at the same time. Several weeks prior to the actual running of a handicap race, the racing secretary will carefully examine the past performances of all eligible horses for the race. The racing secretary will focus his/her attention on such factors as age, sex, money earned, previous weight assignments, types of races, the number of wins, and the overall racing record. Sometimes in a handicap race, you will find stake-caliber horses stepping down in class and allowance horses stepping up in class.

At this point, the reader should also be aware of the overnight handicap. This type of handicap race is one in which the entries have to be posted with the racing secretary 72 hours or less before the first race of the day on which the overnight handicap is scheduled to run.

STAKE RACE: The stake race is the highest plateau of racing. The term "stake" is an abbreviation of the term "sweepstake." Owners are required to post a series of eligibility fees as well as a final entry fee. All the contributing fees become part of the overall purse, to which the racetrack itself adds money toward the final guaranteed amount.

There are various types of stake races, which are run under a variety of conditions. Some stake races are run as handicaps in which weight is assigned according to the racing secretary's evaluation of each horse. Other stake races are run under allowance conditions in which weight is applied according to the amount of purse money earned by each horse. Those with successful racing records will be assigned higher weight than those with less impressive records. Finally, there are the weight-for-age stake races in which each horse is assigned a prescribed weight set forth by the rules of the Jockey Club.

The high-class stake races are distinguished from other stake races by a grading system. The Thoroughbred Breeders and Owners Association developed a grade system for North American stake races according to their importance. Named stake races are either grade 1, 2, or 3 (for example, the Belmont Stakes are graded G-1). This system makes it easier for all concerned to determine which races are the most important races to win. Of all the types of races, the stake and handicap races usually offer the highest amount of purse money. Examples of the various types of races offered at North American racetracks are shown in Figure 12-2.

In addition to the normal types of races offered at a racetrack, there is the match race. A match race is merely a race

12-2. Types of races offered at North American tracks. (Copyright © 2003 by Daily Racing Form, Inc. and Equibase Company. Reprinted with permission.)

between 2 outstanding horses. Match races occurred in America as early as 1820 and were based on the concept of winner take all, which still exists in today's match races. Usually the owners of both horses agree to the location, purse, and distance of the race. Although wagering is usually permitted on match races, the race itself is considered to be more of an exhibition or a public relations event by the racetrack.

12-3. Mobile starting gate. (United States Trotting Association)

Some examples of famous match races held over the years are as follows:

Date	Winner	Opponent	Racetrack	Miles
10-12-1920	Man O' War	Sir Barton	Kenilworth Park	1 1/4
11-01-1938	Seabiscuit	War Admiral	Pimlico	1 3/16
08-31-1955	Nashua	Swaps	Washington Park	1 1/4
07-20-1974	Chris Everett	Miss Musket	Hollywood Park	1 1/4
07-06-1975	Foolish Pleasure	Ruffian	Belmont Park	1 1/4

Standardbred Harness Racing

The types of races mentioned herein are not limited to Thoroughbred racing. In fact, Standardbred harness racing utilizes the same type of races. This type of horseracing is very popular throughout the United States and the world. Harness racing differs from Thoroughbred racing in that Thoroughbreds run or gallop, while Standardbreds must maintain a specific gait. This specific gait refers to either trotting or pacing, which

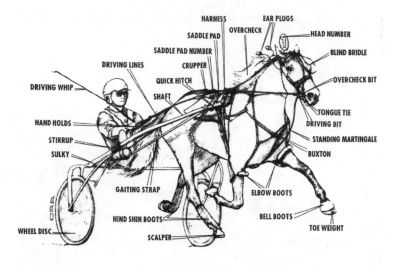

12-4. Equipment commonly worn by the trotter. (United States Trotting Association)

are natural methods of locomotion for the Standardbred harness horse. Standardbreds are guided by a driver seated in sulky, which is a lightweight 2-wheeled cart, instead of being ridden by a jockey in a saddle. Standardbred harness racing does not use a stationary starting gate but instead utilizes the mobile gate to start races.

The mobile gate consists of a set of metal wings or extensions at right angles to the chassis of the automobile on which they are mounted. This barrier prevents any horse from getting ahead of the starting gate. The horses line up behind the gate in their respective post positions and move with gradually increasing speed to the starting point. The wings are then folded against the side of the car and the vehicle is accelerated, leaving a clear passage for the horses (Figure 12-3).

The name "Standardbred" was derived from the standard by which all horses were judged on their ability to trot or pace a distance of 1 mile in 2 minutes and 30 seconds. The average Standardbred is about 15 hands in height, which is con-

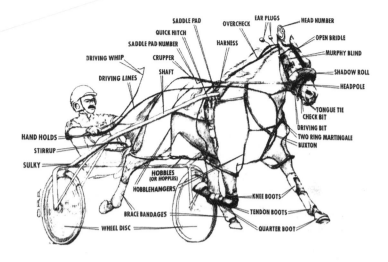

12-5. Equipment commonly worn by the pacer. (United States Trotting Association)

siderably shorter than a Thoroughbred. The Standardbred also lacks the quality and refinement of a Thoroughbred but does have a powerful build featuring a long back with sloping shoulders and short, sturdy legs. While the tendency to trot or pace is inbred in most Standardbred horses, the ability to maintain a specific gait at high speeds and over a distance of ground requires a great deal of training as well as specialized equipment. A trotter is a Standardbred that races with a diagonally gaited motion. The left front and right rear legs move forward at the same time, followed by the right front and left rear legs (Figure 12-4).

A Standardbred pacer, on the other hand, moves with both left legs moving forward in unison, followed by both right legs moving forward. This movement is referred to as a lateral gait (Figure 12-5). A pacer is considered slightly faster and is able to get away faster at the start. Trotting races are restricted to only trotters, and pacing races are restricted to only pacers.

RACES AND PLACES

There are thousands of Thoroughbred races every year around the country and more than 100 tracks that feature this type of racing. Some tracks and races have achieved legendary status. Racing fans should make a point of visiting some of these historic tracks or attending one of the great annual races. Like baseball's older stadiums and team rivalries that are steeped in lore, there are particular races and places that those who enjoy horseracing consider to be among the treasures of American sport.

The Triple Crown

The most prestigious races the American turf has to offer are the famous Triple Crown races. The Triple Crown consists of the Kentucky Derby, which is run on the first Saturday of May; the Preakness Stakes, which is run 2 weeks after the Kentucky Derby; and the Belmont Stakes, which is run 3 weeks after the Preakness. All 3 races are restricted to 3 year olds of either sex. The term "Triple Crown" was believed to be originally coined in the late 1920s by *The Daily Racing Form* turf writer Charles Hatton. However, it was the *New York Times* writer Bryan Field who first printed the term after Gallant Fox won the Belmont Stakes back in 1930. Since 1919, only 11 Thoroughbreds have won the Triple Crown.

Triple Crown Winners

2015 American Pharoah

1978 Affirmed

1977 Seattle Slew

1973 Secretariat

1948 Citation

1946 Assault

1943 Count Fleet

1941 Whirlaway

1937 War Admiral

1935 Omaha

1930 Gallant

1919 Sir Barton

KENTUCKY DERBY

The first Kentucky Derby was run at the Louisville Jockey Club in 1875. The track later became known as Churchill Downs. Churchill Downs is world famous for its twin spires found atop the grandstand roof. Although 3 American racetracks are older than Churchill Downs, the Kentucky track is the only track that has operated throughout its entire existence. The Kentucky Derby is the only classic race that has been run without interruption since its inception in 1875. The inaugural value of the purse was $2,850.00 and has now become one of the richest 3-year-old races in the world with an estimated purse of $2 million in 2005. In 1973, Secretariat established a new record of 1:59 2/5 for the 1 1/4-mile distance. His time still stands as the fastest Kentucky Derby ever run. The race is traditionally run on the first Saturday in May each year.

Traditions of the Kentucky Derby include:

The official flower—Red rose

The official trophy—Kentucky Derby Trophy

The official drink—Mint julep

The official song—"My Old Kentucky Home"

The official distance—1 1/4 miles

Purse (2004)—$1 million

PREAKNESS STAKES

The second jewel of the Triple Crown is held annually on the third Saturday in May. The race was named after a colt owned by Milton H. Sanford back in 1870. The first running took place on May 23, 1873, at Pimlico Racecourse with a purse valued at $1,000.00. At the time, Pimlico was owned and operated by the Maryland Jockey Club. The race was originally contested at 1 1/8 miles up until 1925 when it was lengthened to 1 3/16 miles. A Preakness tradition practiced each year is the painting of the colors of the winner's silks on a weather vane, which is located on top of the Preakness Presentation Stand at Pimlico. In 1996, Louis Quatorze posted the fastest Preakness time of 1:53.43 for the 1 3/16-mile distance. Today, the gross value of the Preakness Stakes is set at $1,000,000.00

Traditions of the Preakness Stakes include:

The official flower—Black-eyed Susan

The official trophy—The woodland vase

The official drink—The black-eyed Susan

The official song—"Maryland My Maryland"

The official distance—1 3/16 miles

Purse (2004)—$1 million

BELMONT STAKES

The final jewel of the Triple Crown is the Belmont Stakes. The race was named after August Belmont I, a prominent Thoroughbred owner and president of the American Jockey Club. The first running took place in 1867 at Jerome Park, which was located in the Bronx section of New York City. The distance at the time was 1 5/8 miles. In 1867, the inaugural running of the Belmont Stakes offered a purse valued at $1,850.00. Today, the Belmont Stakes offers a purse valued at $1,000,000.00. In 1890, the race was held at Morris Park, which was also located in the Bronx, at a reduced distance of 1 3/8 miles. In 1905, the race was moved to Belmont Park located on Long Island, New York. In 1926, the distance was established at 1 1/2 miles and has remained the same till this day. In 1973, Secretariat won the Belmont Stakes and the Triple Crown by a record 31 lengths and set a world record of 2:24 for the 1 1/2-mile distance.

Traditions of the Belmont Stakes include:

The official flower—White carnation

The official trophy—Belmont Memorial Challenge Trophy

The official drink—Belmont breeze

The official song—"New York, New York"

The official distance—1 1/2 miles

Purse (2004)—$1 million

Breeders' Cup World Thoroughbred Championship

In addition to the Triple Crown Races in the spring, the American turf offers the Breeders' Cup World Thoroughbred Championship in the fall of each year. Some view the Breeders' Cup races as the World Series of horseracing. Mr. John R. Gaines, a prominent Thoroughbred breeder, is responsible for creating the concept of the Breeders' Cup series back in the early 1980s.

The Breeders' Cup races are based on sex, age, distance, and surface (dirt or grass). Whereas the Triple Crown is limited to only 3 year olds, the Breeders' Cup is open to all. Today, The Breeders' Cup World Championship consists of a total of

8 races with total purses amounting to $14 million. The schedule of races on Breeders' Cup Day consists of the following:

Breeders' Cup Turf: $2 million, for 3 year olds and up, 1 1/2 miles on turf.

Breeders' Cup Juvenile: $1.5 million, for 2-year-old colts and geldings, 1 1/8 miles on dirt.

Breeders' Cup Fillies and Mares Turf: $1 million, for 3 year olds and up, 1 1/4 miles on turf.

Breeders' Cup Sprint: $1 million, for 3 year olds and up, 6 furlongs on dirt.

Breeders' Cup Mile: $1.5 million, for 3 year olds and up, 1 mile on turf.

Breeders' Cup Juvenile Fillies: $1 million, for 2-year-old fillies, 1 1/8 miles on dirt.

Breeders' Cup Distaff: $2 million, for 3 year olds and up, fillies and mares, 1 1/8 miles on dirt.

Breeders' Cup Classic: $4 million, for 3 year olds and up, 1 1/4 miles on dirt.

The Breeders' Cup brings the best horses in the world together on a single day in the fall of each year. The first Breeders' Cup races were held in 1984 at Hollywood Park in California. The championship event is held at a different location each year. In addition to Hollywood Park, past sites have included Belmont Park and Aqueduct Racetrack in New York; Arlington Park in Illinois; Churchill Downs in Kentucky; Santa Anita Park in California; Gulfstream Park in Florida; Woodbine Racetrack in Ontario, Canada; and Lone Star Park in Texas.

The results of the Breeders' Cup World Thoroughbred Championship has a definite bearing at the end of the racing year in determining Horse of the Year as well as division champions.

13-1. The Breeders' Cup trophy. (Reprinted with permission of Breeders' Cup, Ltd.)

The winner of each of the Breeders' Cup races is presented the official Breeders' Cup trophy. The trophy is a replica of the Torrie horse sculptured by Giovanni da Bologna in the late 1580s (Figure 13-1).

Horses for Courses

There are many Thoroughbreds that have become prominent and have made their mark at certain racetracks throughout the country. Professional handicappers refer to these individuals as horses for courses. These are horses that have won numerous races and have loyal fans at a particular racetrack in which their connections call home.

Some examples of these outstanding individuals include the following horses:

SEABISCUIT: He is best remembered for his match race victory over War Admiral at Pimlico in 1938. Sportswriters would say that Seabiscuit "would go anywhere a railroad track took him" for a race. During his racing career, he traveled all over the country, but California and Santa Anita racetrack were considered his home. As a 2 year old in 1935, Seabiscuit raced 35 times, which is more than most horses race during their entire careers. He had raced 17 times before winning his first race. In 1937, he finished second by a nose to a horse named Rosemont in the $100,000.00 Santa Anita Handicap, the world's richest race at the time. After his match race victory over Triple Crown winner War Admiral, Seabiscuit was voted 1938 Horse of the Year.

During that same year, he finished second by a nose for the second consecutive time to a horse named Stagehand in the Santa Anita Handicap. He became known to racing fans across America as the Californian ugly duckling. After a lay-off from racing for a year due to a leg injury, Seabiscuit was prepared for the 1940 running of the Santa Anita Handicap. His comeback included 2 races at Santa Anita where he finished third in one and sixth in another. The 7-year-old Seabiscuit was assigned 130 pounds for the Santa Anita Handicap. Finally, after 2 near misses, Seabiscuit finished first in his last race to win the 1940 Santa Anita Handicap. His racing career consisted of 89 starts with 33 wins, 15 seconds, and 13 thirds, with a total lifetime earnings of $437,730.00. He was permanently retired to Mr. Charles Howard's Ridgewood farm in California until his death in 1947. A statute of Seabiscuit was erected in his memory at Santa Anita Park and remains there today as a tribute to this great horse.

SILKY SULLIVAN: The come-from-behind horse. In 1957, the entire country was talking about the West-Coast wonder horse Silky Sullivan. As a 2 year old, he had won the 1-mile Golden Gate Futurity after trailing the field by some 27 lengths at Golden Gate Fields racetrack in northern California. As a 3 year old in 1958, he won the Santa Anita Derby in the same manner after trailing the field by some 28 lengths. Silky

Sullivan retired with 12 victories in 27 starts. Each year on St. Patrick's Day, Silky Sullivan was paraded before his fans at Golden Gate Fields racetrack, the site of his first important win. He was always a special favorite with the fans at Golden Gate Fields. The weekday crowd of 18,532 fans who came to see him at Golden Gate was an attendance record that stood for 25 years. After his death in 1977, Silky Sullivan was buried on the grounds of Golden Gate Fields racetrack

KELSO: "Here comes Kelso" was the announcer's call each time this gelding began to run in a race. Kelso raced primarily in New York and was a huge hit with the New York racing fans. He raced up until he was 9 years old. His racing career consisted of 39 wins in 63 starts with total career earnings of $1,977,896.00. Kelso was voted Horse of the Year for 5 straight years (1960–1964). At Belmont Park in New York, he won the Jockey Club Gold Cup 5 times and the Woodward Stakes 3 times. In 1983, the 26-year-old Kelso led the post parade of the Jockey Club Gold Cup at Belmont Park, a race that he had won 5 straight times (1960–1964). The following day at Belmont, Kelso suffered an attack of colic and died. Kelso was inducted into the Racing Hall of Fame in 1967.

RUFFIAN: This superstar ran 10 races against other fillies and won them all with little effort. She won the Triple Crown for fillies and set track records even as a 2 year old. She had earned $313,428.00 in her short career in 1974 and 1975. Most of her races were won at Belmont Park, where she had many loyal fans. She was a powerful and graceful runner. She had 11 starts with 10 wins; her only defeat came against the colt Foolish Pleasure—the 1975 Kentucky Derby winner. The famous match race on July 6, 1975, between the best filly Ruffian and the best colt Foolish Pleasure ended with Ruffian injuring her ankle during the running of the race and ending her career as well as her life. After hours of surgery, veterinarians were unable to keep Ruffian quiet after she came out of he anesthetic. She began to panic and struggle; in the process, the surgical cast came off, and she undid the surgical repair of her ankle. She was humanely euthanized on July 7, 1975, and was buried near a flagpole on the infield of Belmont Park. When she was buried, her head was pointed toward the finish line.

FOURSTARDAVE: This remarkable gelding became known as the Sultan of Saratoga. He raced from 1987 to 1995 and won a race at Saratoga Race Course for 8 consecutive years. Fourstardave was very popular with the Saratoga racing fans. He was 9 years old when he was retired from racing in 1995 as the leading New York–bred money earner. Fourstardave's racing career consisted of 100 starts with 21 wins, 18 seconds, and 16 thirds, with total earnings of $1,636,737.00. He succumbed to a heart attack and died on October 15, 2002, at Belmont Park when he was preparing for an exhibition for New York–bred horses. Saratoga Race Course has named a race in his honor, which is traditionally run on Travers Day in late August.

SMARTY JONES: Smarty Jones was dubbed "the little horse that could" by his fans at Philadelphia Park. Before he raced, he miraculously survived a serious head injury due to an accident in the starting gate, which could have ended his career as well as his life. In 2003, Smarty Jones started his racing career at Philadelphia Park, a relatively small local racetrack in Bensalem, Pennsylvania. As a 2 year old, he won 2 races there, including the Pennsylvania Nursery Stakes. As a 3 year old, he went on to win 8 graded stake races in 2004, including the Kentucky Derby and Preakness Stakes. In his attempt to win racing's Triple Crown, his only defeat came in the Belmont Stakes. Before a record New York crowd of 120,139 fans, Smarty Jones finished second, beaten by 1 length by a horse named Birdstone. In the summer of 2004, Smarty Jones was retired from racing with a record of 9 starts with 8 wins and 1 second and total earnings of $7,613,155.00. Smarty Jones is presently standing stud in Kentucky at Three Chimney Farm with a stud fee of $100,000.00.

North American Tracks and Major Thoroughbred Races

Throughout North America, there are approximately 126 racetracks in operation. Each day these racetracks offer live racing to the betting public attending their facility or to those receiving a satellite simulcast signal. The following is merely a sample of some of the major races offered throughout the year.

ARKANSAS

OAKLAWN PARK: Hot Springs
Total real estate: 120 acres
Seating: 26,200
Layout: 1-mile dirt track
Major races: *Arkansas Derby* ($500,000.00 purse, 1 1/8 miles on dirt, for 3 year olds, in April)
Apple Blossom Handicap ($500,000.00 purse, 1 1/16 miles on dirt, for fillies and mares, 4 year olds and up, in April)

CALIFORNIA

DEL MAR: Del Mar
Total real estate: 350 acres
Seating: 14,304
Layout: 1 1/4-mile dirt track and 1 1/8-mile turf course
Major races: *Pacific Classic Stakes* ($1 million purse, 1 1/4 miles on dirt, for 3 year olds and up, in August)

SANTA ANITA: Arcadia
Total real estate: 323 acres
Seating: 19,249

Layout: 1 1/4-mile dirt track and 1 3/4-mile turf course
Major races: *Santa Anita Handicap* ($1 million purse, 1 1/4 miles on dirt, for 4 year olds and up, in March)
Santa Anita Derby ($750,000.00 purse, 1 1/8 miles on dirt, for 3 year olds, in April)

HOLLYWOOD PARK: Inglewood
Total real estate: 240 acres
Seating: 10,000
Layout: 1 1/8-mile dirt track and 1-mile turf course
Major races: *Hollywood Gold Cup Stakes* ($750,000.00 purse, 1 1/4 miles on dirt, for 3 year olds and up, in July)
California Stakes ($500,000.00 purse, 1 1/8 miles on dirt, for 3 year olds and up, in June)
Hollywood Derby ($500,000.00 purse, 1 1/16 miles on turf, for 3 year olds, in December)

DELAWARE

DELAWARE PARK: Stanton
Total real estate: Not available
Seating: 17,750
Layout: 1 1/4-mile dirt track and 7-furlong turf course
Major races: *Delaware Handicap* ($600,000.00 purse, 1 1/4 miles on dirt, for fillies and mares, 3 year olds and up, in July)

FLORIDA

GULFSTREAM PARK: Hallandale
Total real estate: 56 acres
Seating: 20,300
Layout: 1-mile dirt track and 7-furlong turf course
Major races: *Florida Derby* ($1 million purse, 1 1/8 miles on dirt, for 3 year olds, in March)
Donn Handicap ($500,000.00 purse, 1 1/8 miles on dirt, for 3 year olds and up, in February)

ILLINOIS

ARLINGTON INTERNATIONAL RACE COURSE: Arlington Heights
Total real estate: 325 acres
Seating: 35,000
Layout: 1 1/8-mile dirt track and 1-mile turf course
Major races: *Arlington Million Stakes* ($1 million purse, 1 1/4 miles on turf, for 3 year olds and up, in August)
Beverly D. Stakes ($700,000.00 purse, 1 3/16 miles on turf, for fillies and mares, 3 year olds and up, in August)

HAWTHORNE RACE COURSE: Cicero
Total real estate: 119 acres
Seating: 18,000
Layout: 1-mile dirt track and 7-furlong and 148-foot turf courses
Major races: *Illinois Derby* ($500,000.00 purse, 1 1/8 miles on dirt, for 3 year olds, in April)
Hawthorne Gold Cup Handicap ($500,000.00 purse, 1 1/16 miles on dirt, for fillies and mares, 3 year olds and up, in April)

INDIANA

HOOSIER PARK: Anderson
Total real estate: 105 acres
Seating: 15,000
Layout: 7-furlong dirt track
Major races: *Indiana Derby* ($400,000.00 purse, 1 1/16 miles on dirt, for 3 year olds, in October)

IOWA

PRAIRIE MEADOWS: Altoona
Total real estate: 233 acres
Seating: 7,000
Layout: 1-mile dirt track
Major races: *Prairie Meadows Cornhuskers Breeders' Cup*

Handicap ($400,000.00 purse, 1 1/8 miles on dirt, for 3 year olds and up, in July)

KENTUCKY

CHURCHILL DOWNS: Louisville
Total real estate: 147 acres
Seating: 48,500
Layout: 1-mile dirt track and 7-furlong turf course
Major races: *Kentucky Derby* (see the description of the Triple Crown races in this chapter)
Stephen Foster Handicap ($750,000.00 purse, 1 1/8 miles on dirt, for 3 year olds and up, in June)
Kentucky Oaks ($500,000.00 purse, 1 1/8 miles on dirt, for 3-year-old fillies, in May)

KEENELAND RACE COURSE: Lexington
Total real estate: 907 acres
Seating: 7,000
Layout: 1 1/16-mile dirt track and 7 1/2-furlong turf course
Major races: *Bluegrass Stakes* ($750,000.00 purse, 1 1/8 miles on dirt, for 3 year olds, in April)
Shadwell Keeneland Turf Mile ($600,000.00 purse, 1 mile on turf, for 3 year olds and up, in October)
Ashland Stakes ($500,000.00 purse, 1 1/16 miles on dirt, for 3-year-old fillies, in April)

TURFWAY PARK: Florence
Total real estate: 197 acres
Seating: 10,000
Layout: 1-mile dirt track
Major races: *Lanes' End Stakes* ($500,000.00 purse, 1 1/8 miles on dirt, for 3 year olds, in March)

LOUISIANA

DELTA DOWNS: Vinton
Total real estate: 240 acres

Seating: Not available
Layout: 6-furlong dirt track
Major races: *Delta Jackpot Stakes* ($500,000.00 purse, 1 mile on dirt, for 2 year olds, in December)

FAIR GROUNDS: New Orleans
Total real estate: 145 acres
Seating: 11,000
Layout: 1-mile dirt track and 7-furlong turf course
Major races: *Louisiana Derby* ($750,000.00 purse, 1 1/16 miles on dirt, for 3 year olds, in March)
Explosive Bid Handicap ($650,000.00 purse, 1 1/8 miles on turf, for 4 year olds and up, in March)
New Orleans Handicap ($500,000.00 purse, 1 1/8 miles on dirt, for 4 year olds and up, in March)

LOUISIANA DOWNS: Bossier City
Total real estate: 350 acres
Seating: 17,240
Layout: 1-mile dirt track and 7-furlong and 50-foot turf course
Major races: *Super Derby* ($500,000.00 purse, 1 1/8 miles on dirt, for 3 year olds, in September)

MARYLAND

PIMLICO: Baltimore
Total real estate: 140 acres
Seating: 13,047
Layout: 1-mile dirt track and 7-furlong turf course
Major races: *Preakness Stakes* (see the description of the Triple Crown races in this chapter)
Pimlico Special ($600,000.00 purse, 1 1/16 miles on dirt, for 3 year olds and up, in May)

MASSACHUSETTS

SUFFOLK DOWNS: East Boston

Total real estate: 190 acres
Seating: 9,505
Layout: 1-mile dirt track and 7-furlong turf course
Major races: *Massachusetts Handicap* ($500,000.00 purse, 1 1/8 miles on dirt, for 3 year olds and up, in June)

NEW JERSEY

MONMOUTH PARK: Oceanport
Total real estate: 500 acres
Seating: 18,000
Layout: 1-mile dirt track and 7-furlong turf course
Major races: *Haskell Invitational Handicap* ($1 million purse, 1 1/8 miles on dirt, for 3 year olds, in August)
United Nations Handicap ($500,000.00 purse, 1 3/8 miles on turf, for 3 year olds and up, in July)

NEW YORK

AQUEDUCT: Ozone Park
Total real estate: 192 acres
Seating: 17,000
Layout: 1 1/8-mile outer track, 1-mile winter inner track, and 7-furlong turf course
Major races: *Wood Memorial Stakes* ($750,000.00 purse, 1 1/8 miles on dirt, for 3 year olds, in April)
Cigar Mile Handicap ($350,000.00 purse, 1 mile on dirt, for 3 year olds and up, in November)

BELMONT PARK: Belmont
Total real estate: 430 acres
Seating: 32,941
Layout: 1 1/2-mile dirt track, 1 5/16-mile outer turf course, and 1 3/16-mile inner turf course
Major races: *Belmont Stakes* (see the description of the Triple Crown races in this chapter)
Jockey Club Gold Cup ($1 million purse, 1 1/4 miles on dirt,

for 3 year olds and up, in September)

Metropolitan Handicap ($750,000.00 purse, 1 mile on dirt, for 3 year olds and up, in May)

SARATOGA RACE COURSE: Saratoga Springs
Total real estate: 350 acres
Seating: 18,000
Layout: 1 1/8-mile dirt track, 1-mile outer turf course, and 7-furlong inner turf course
Major races: *Travers Stakes* ($1 million purse, 1 1/4 miles on dirt, for 3 year olds, in August)
Alabama Stakes ($750,000.00 purse, 1 1/4 miles on dirt, for 3-year-old fillies, in August)
Whitney Stakes ($750,000.00 purse, 1 1/8 miles on dirt, for 3 year olds and up, in August)
Jim Dandy Stakes ($500,000.00 purse, 1 1/8 miles on dirt, for 3 year olds, in August)

PENNSYLVANIA

PHILADELPHIA PARK: Bensalem
Total real estate: 417 acres
Seating: 8,700
Layout: 1-mile dirt track and 7-furlong turf course
Major races: *Pennsylvania Derby* ($500,000.00 purse, 1 1/8 miles on dirt, for 3 year olds, in September)

TEXAS

LONE STAR PARK: Grand Prairie
Total real estate: 315 acres
Seating: 12,000
Layout: 1-mile dirt track and 7-furlong turf course
Major races: *Lone Star Derby* ($500,000.00 purse, 1 1/8 miles on dirt, for 3 year olds, in May)
Lone Star Park Handicap ($300,000.00 purse, 1 1/16 miles on dirt, for 3 year olds and up, in May)

Virginia

Colonial Downs: New Kent
Total real estate: 345 acres
Seating: 6,000
Layout: 1 1/4-mile dirt track and 7 1/2-furlong turf course
Major races: *Virginia Derby* ($500,000.00 purse, 1 1/4 miles on turf, for 3 year olds, in July)

West Virginia

Mountaineer Race Track: Chester
Total real estate: 1,945 acres
Seating: 7,400
Layout: 1-mile dirt track and 7-furlong turf course
Major races: *West Virginia Derby* ($500,000.00 purse, 1 1/8 mile on dirt, for 3 year olds, in August)

Canada

Woodbine Race Course: Rexdale, Ontario
Total real estate: 650 acres
Seating: 18,996
Layout: 1-mile dirt track and 1 1/2-mile turf course
Major races: *Canadian International Stakes* ($1.5 million purse, 1 1/2 miles on turf, for 3 year olds and up, in September)
Queen's Plate Stakes ($1 million purse, 1 1/4 miles on dirt, for 3-year-old Canadian-bred horses, in June)
E. P. Taylor Stakes ($750,000.00 purse, 1 1/4 miles on turf, for 3-year-old fillies and mares, in September)

Fort Erie Race Track: Fort Erie, Ontario
Total real estate: Not available
Seating: 4,000
Layout: 1-mile dirt track and 7-furlong turf course
Major races: *Prince of Wales Stakes* ($500,000.00 purse, 1 3/16 miles on dirt, 3-year-old Canadian-bred horses, in July)

14

OWNERSHIP

The racehorse owner is truly the backbone of the industry. The modern owner or owners of a racehorse are the type that makes sound businesslike decisions concerning the horses in their stable. This new breed of owner will demand a full account of every dollar invested in their racing venture. Communication with the trainer, farm manager, accountant, and racing officials is essential. Long gone are the days when owners were asked to outlay large sums of money with little participation in the decision-making process that is involved in horseracing.

Most owners enjoy the sport of horseracing and have a genuine love for the horse. They derive a great deal of pleasure visiting the stable in the morning as well as attending the races in the afternoon. The owner who becomes part of this unique sport with the sole purpose of making money is soon disappointed.

The owner of a racehorse is responsible for the following expenses:

Purchase price of the horse
Trainer's fee
Veterinarian fees (including dentistry)
Farrier (blacksmith) fees
Transportation fees

143

Equipment and medications

Insurance premiums

Jockey fees

Entry fees

Owner's license fee

Cost of racing silks

The ownership of a racehorse is a commitment of both money and time. There are no guarantees of success. In fact, the odds are such that an owner will probably be unsuccessful. However, there is always the possibility that a horse will go on to win the Kentucky Derby. For example, the late horse Seattle Slew was purchased for $17,500.00 and became a Triple Crown winner with earnings in excess of $1 million. Some of the everyday problems that occur to a horse that also affect the owner are injuries, illness, and in some cases, death, and owners should understand these risks. Once you become a licensed owner you will be issued a badge and an automobile sticker that allows you free access to the backstretch and clubhouse during the race meets.

There are several ways of becoming a racehorse owner. One may purchase a horse outright either privately or at a public auction. Private purchases allow the purchaser to have the horse examined and X-rayed by a veterinarian. After a final price is agreed upon and paid by the new owner, the new owner should receive a bill of sale, Jockey Club foal certificate, and all veterinary records available on the horse. The bill of sale should identify the horse, including the name and address of both the seller and buyer, terms of the sale, purchase price, date of sale, location of the sale, and any warranties of the sale (Figure 14-1). Potential owners may also attend a public auction sale. There are may different types of auction sales that offer various types of horses to the highest bidder Some auctions specialize in stock such as weanlings, yearlings, 2 year olds, and horses of racing age.

BILL OF SALE

I. _____, residing at _____
_____, in consideration of _____
_____, hereby paid to me by _____
residing at _____, sell to
_____ the following described horse:

Name: _____
Age: _____
Color: _____
Breed: _____
Sex: _____
Size: _____

I hereby covenant that I am the lawful owner of the horse; that I have the right to sell the horse;
and that I will warrant and defend said horse against lawful claims and demands of all persons.
Executed this _____ day of _____, 20 ___ .

_____
Signature of Seller

14-1 Example of an official Thoroughbred bill of sale. (Author)

There is also the dispersal sale in which a farm or stable is selling all of its horses. The potential owner must obtain a sales catalog and analyze the pedigrees and racing records of the horses listed. A physical inspection of the horses offered is essential in order to detect any infirmities. Unless you are a knowledgeable horse person, it would be best to deal with a professional trainer or a bloodstock agent when attending an auction sale.

Another means of acquiring a racehorse is through a claiming race. In this case, you or your trainer must place a claim prior to the race for a designated amount. For example, if the race is a $25,000.00 claiming race, all the horses entered are eligible to be claimed for $25,000.00. However claiming a horse may be restricted to owners who have raced a horse at the present meeting in the claimant's name. This requirement may be waived if you are a new owner and you don't already own a racehorse or you are an owner whose stable has been eliminated due to claiming, stable fire, or other hazard. Under these circumstances you may request a steward's certificate of claim. Another requirement for claiming a horse is to have sufficient funds on deposit with the racetrack bookkeeper. One must also complete and sign an official claim card (Figure 14-2). All claim cards must be deposited in the claim box 15 minutes before the start of the race. Once a horse is claimed from a race, it is not permitted to start for a period of 30 days from the date of claim for less than 25% more than the amount for which it was claimed.

Another method of ownership is for one to enter into a partnership. There is an old saying in the horseracing industry that states "It is better to own part of a good horse than to own all of a bad horse." In this type of ownership, you become a partner with one or more individuals in the ownership of a racehorse. As a partner, you are only responsible for the expenses of your designated percentage share of ownership. If your ownership percentage share is 25%, then you are only responsible for 25% of all the expenses incurred each month. A partnership consisting of several individuals may race under one stable name. Uniting the partnership under one stable name makes it that much easier for the racetrack, the trainer, and racing commission in dealings concerning the stable. Usually one of the partners is designated as the managing partner to whom all correspondence and invoices are directed. Naturally, any purse money earned by the racehorse owned in partnership is distributed among the partners according to their percentage share of ownership.

Taking racehorse ownership a step further than a general partnership is the limited liability company (LLC). The limited liability company allows a large number of people to share ownership in one or more racehorses by combining the features of a corporation and a partnership. Limited liability

KNOWLEDGE: A good trainer is one who is han
horses in his or her charge. Trainers should b

CLAIM BLANK

Thoroughbred RACE COURSE

....20......

TO THE CLERK OF THE RACE COURSE:

I hereby claim the horse..from the
Print

.................................race of this date, for the sum of $...........................plus
any State Tax assessed, under and subject to the RULES OF RACING.

OWNER ....

Per ....
Authorized Agent

14-2. An official claim card. (Author)

companies are now authorized in most racing states and are required to file annual reports to the state business authority. They are not recognized by the Internal Revenue Service as a separate venture. The limited liability company is not required to report or file any tax reports to the Internal Revenue Service. However, income and expense statements must be reported to the Internal Revenue Service by all the individual members of the limited liability company on their personal yearly tax returns.

Another alternative to ownership that is very common in the horseracing industry is leasing. The lessor is the person who actually owns the horse, and the lessee is the person leasing the horse from the owner for racing purposes. The major advantage to leasing is that the lessee merely leases the horse for a specified amount of time. There is no lifetime commitment to the animal. When the lease period has terminated, the lessee's financial interest is also terminated.

During the lease period, the lessee is fully responsible for all expenses incurred as well as the general well-being of the horse. It is recommended that a written lease agreement be signed by both parties specifying the responsibility of each party during the lease period. Horses may be leased for racing and breeding purposes.

Racehorse ownership may also start out as a breeding venture. A person or group may purchase a broodmare and have the mare bred to a particular stallion. When the foal is born, it is the official property of the owner of the mare. The owner of the mare is also designated as the breeder of the foal. It will be 2 years before the horse will be able to race. During this time, the owner/breeder is responsible for all expenses incurred in maintaining both mare and foal. When the foal becomes a yearling, the breaking and gentling process begins. The horse is introduced to the saddle and bridle as well as the weight of a rider on its back. For this purpose, it may be necessary to send the yearling to a training center where it is allowed to develop and become accustomed to a starting gate and other racetrack procedures. As a 2 year old, the horse becomes eligible to race. It is easy to comprehend the large amount of expenditures involved in breeding and developing a racehorse until it is ready to race.

During this 2-year period, the owner/breeder must bear the following major expenses:

Purchase price of the broodmare
Stud fee
Monthly boarding fees
Initial breaking and training fee
Racetrack training fees
Veterinary fees
Insurance fees

As the owner/breeder, you must now select a professional trainer to train your horse while at the racetrack. Some of the traits that the owner/breeder must look for when selecting a trainer are as follows:

KNOWLEDGE: A good trainer is one who is hands on with the horses in his or her charge. Trainers should be able to detect ailments, administer medication, apply bandages, practice good nutrition, and be able to determine when a horse is in good physical condition.

COMMUNICATION: Trainers should be in constant communication with owners. They should update owners on the progress of their horse's training on a regular basis. They should not refrain from telling owners the truth about any problems that their horses may encounter. Their job is to keep owners well informed so that they are able to make intelligent decisions concerning the success of their stable.

CONSISTENCY: The trainer should exhibit a high win and in-the-money percentage.

ACCOUNTABILITY: The trainer should be accountable for all of the stable's operations. There should be no excuses for a horse's poor performance or that of the stable employees.

PROFESSIONALISM: Overall, the trainer must provide his/her clients with the best possible service with honesty and integrity.

As a newly licensed owner of a racehorse, you must now select the colors for your silks. They are worn as a shirt by the jockey each time the owner's horse races. The practice of each owner having individual silks was established in 1762 in Newmarket, England. In America, the Jockey Club is responsible for issuing silks to owners. They were originally made of silk, but today they are usually made of nylon and cost approximately $150.00, depending on the design. Colors and designs on the jacket, sleeves, and cap must be approved by the Jockey Club. In some states, logos and designs that can be interpreted as advertising are not permitted. However, there are some states that are allowing commercial advertising on silks, saddlecloths, and jockey pants in order to entice corporate sponsors to horseracing. Another duty of the Jockey Club is the naming of Thoroughbreds. As an owner of an unnamed Thoroughbred, you will have to apply for a name for your horse as it will appear on the official foal certificate. The name can be no more than 18 characters; this includes spaces and punctuation marks. The name cannot be the same as a famous horse living or deceased. For example, you cannot use the name Man O' War. Commercial brand names are also prohibited by the Jockey Club registry.

In addition to purse money earned by horses, owners and breeders may earn additional funds as part of a state breeding and development fund. An owner or breeder may decide to join a state breeding association and take part in the lucrative breeding incentive awards to promote state-bred horses. The state breeding association usually maintains a registry of state-bred and state-based stallions. A breeder of a registered state-bred horse receives a cash award every time his/her horse earns prize money in a race. An owner of a registered state-bred horse is also awarded money when the horse earns purse money in open races. An open race is one in which entries consist of horses that were bred and foaled in states other than the state where the racetrack is located. There are also state-bred races in which the entries are restricted to only those horses that were bred, foaled, and registered in the state where racing is being conducted. Each state that conducts pari-mutuel wagering on horses may also have a state-bred program. A sample of some states that offer lucrative financial incentives for their state-bred owners and breeders are California, New York, Kentucky, Maryland, Pennsylvania, Illinois, and Arizona.

State-bred programs are usually funded by a percentage of the state tax revenue obtained from the pari-mutuel handle at the state's racetrack(s). The 4 basic ingredients of any state-bred program include monetary awards for owners of state-bred horses, restricted races for state-bred horses, monetary awards for breeders of successful state-bred horses, and monetary awards for stallion owners.

Finally, the owner should become familiar with the rules and regulations of racing administered by the state racing commission and racing association conducting a particular race meeting. Every owner should stay within their financial means and not allow greed to enter into the process of decision making.

APPENDIX A

Parts of the Horse

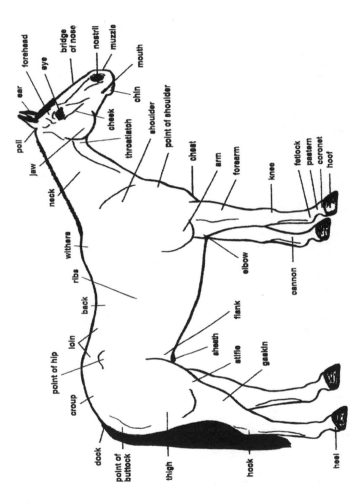

APPENDIX B

North American Pari-mutuel Racetracks

Abd – The Downs at Albuquerque, NM – abqdowns.com
AP – Arlington Park, IL – arlingtonpark.com
Aqu – Aqueduct, NY* – nyra.com/aqueduct
ArP – *Arapahoe Park, CO – wembleyusa.com/arapahoe
AsD – *Assiniboia Downs, Man, Canada – assiniboiadowns.com
Att – Atlantic City, NJ
Bel – Belmont Park, NY – nyra.com/belmont
Beu – Beulah Park, OH – beulahpark.com
BGD – *Blue Grass Downs, KY
BM – Bay Meadows, CA – baymeadows.com
Bmf – Bay Meadows Fair, CA – caltairs.com
Bol – *Boise, ID (Les Bois Park)
BRD – *Blue Ribbon Downs, OK – blueribbondowns.net
Cby – Canterbury Park, MN – canterburypark.com
CD – Churchill Downs, KY – kentuckyderby.com
Cls – *Columbus, NE
Cnl – Colonial Downs, Va. – colonialdowns.com
Crc – Calder Race Course, FL – calderracecourse.com
CT – *Charles Town, WV – ctownraces.com
DeD – *Delta Downs, LA – deltadowns.com
DeP – Desert Park, BC, Canada
Del – Delaware Park, DE – delpark.com
Dmr – Del Mar, CA – dmtc.com
ElP – Ellis Park, KY – ellisparkracing.com
EmD – Emerald Downs, WA – emdowns.com
EvD – *Evangeline Downs, LA – evangelinedowns.com
Fai – Fair Hill, MD
FE – Fort Erie, Ont. Canada
Fer – Ferndale, CA
FG – Fair Grounds, LA – fgno.com
FL – Finger Lakes, NY – fingerlakesracetrack.com
FMT – *Fair Meadows, OK (Tulsa State Fair)
Fno – Fresno, CA
Fen – Fonner Park, NE – fonnerpark.com
FP – Fairmount Park, IL – fairmountpark.com
Fpx – *Fairplex (Pomona), CA – fairplex.com
Fs – Flagstaff, AZ

GF – *Great Falls, MT
GG – *Golden Gate Fields, CA – ggfields.com
GLD – – Great Lakes Downs, MI – greatlakesdowns.com
GP – Gulfstream Park, FL – gulfstreampark.com
GrP – *Grants Pass, OR
GS – Garden State Park, NJ – gspark.com
HaP – *Harbor Park, WA
Haw – Hawthorne, IL
Hia – Hialeah Park, FL – hialeahpark.com
Hol – Hollywood Park, CA – hollywoodpark.com
Hoo – Hoosier, IN – hoosierpark.com
Hou – Sam Houston Race Park, TX – shrp.com
HPO – Horsmen's Park, NE – horsemenspark.com
Hst – *Hastings Park, BC, Canada (Formerly Exhibition Park) – hastingspark.com
Kam – *Kamloops, BC, Canada
KD – Kentucky Downs (Formerly Dueling Grounds) – turfway.com/kydowns
Kee – Keeneland, KY – keeneland.com
Kin – *Kin Park, BC, Canada
LA – *Los Alamitos, CA – losalamitos.com
LaD – Louisana Downs, LA – ladowns.com
LnN – *Lincoln State Fair, NE
Lrl – Laurel Race Course, MD – marylandracing.com
LS – Lone Star Park, TX – lonestarpark.com
MD – *Marquis Downs, Sask, Canada – saskatoonex.com
Med – Meadowlands, NJ
Mnr – Mountaineer Park, WV – mtgaming.com
MPM – *Mt Pleasant Meadows, MI
Mth – Monmouth Park, NJ – monmouthpark.com
Nmp – *Northampton, MA
NP – *Northlands Park, Alta, Canada – northlands.com
OP – Oaklawn Park, AK – oaklawn.com
Pen – Penn National, PA – pnrc.com
Pha – Philadelphia Park, PA – philadelphiapark.com
Pim – Pimlico, MD – marylandracing.com
Pla – *Playfair, WA
Pln – Pleasanton, CA

PM – – Portland Meadows, OR – portlandmeadows.com
Pre – *Prescott Downs, AZ
PrM – Prairie Meadows, IA – prairiemeadows.com
RD – River Downs, OH – riverdowns.com
Ret – Retama Park, TX – retamapark.com
Rll – *Rillito, AZ
Rkm – Rockingham Park, NH – rockinghampark.com
RP – Remington Park, OK – remingtonpark.com
Rui – *Ruidoso Downs, NM – ruidownsracing.com
SA – Santa Anita Park, CA – santaanita.com
Sac – Sacramento, CA
Sal – *Salem, OR (Lone Oak)
San – *Sandown Park, BC, Canada
Sar – Saratoga, NY – nyra.com/saratoga
SFe – Santa Fe, NM
SnD – *Sunflower Downs, BC Canada
Sol – *Solano (Vallejo) CA
Spt – *Sportsmans' Park, IL – sportsmanspark.com
SR – Santa Rosa, CA
SRP – Sun Ray Park, NM – sunraygaming.com
Stk – Stockton, CA
StP – *Stampede Park, Alta, Canada
SuD – Sun Downs, WA
Suf – Suffolk Downs, MA – suffolkdowns.com
Sun – Sunland Park, NM – sunland-park.com
Tam – Tampa Bay Downs, FL – tampadowns.com
Tet – Teton (Sandy Downs), ID
Tdn – Thistledown, OH – thistledown.com
Tim – *Timonium, MD
TP – Turfway Park, KY – turfway.com
TuP – Turf Paradise, AZ – turfparadise.com
Wds – Woodlands, KS
WO – Woodbine, Ont. Canada – ojc.com
WRD – Will Rogers Downs, OK – willrogersdowns.com
Wyo – *Wyoming Downs, WY – wyomingdowns.com
YD – –*Yellowstone Downs, MT
YM – –Yakima Meadows, WA

APPENDIX C

How to Read *The Daily Racing Form*

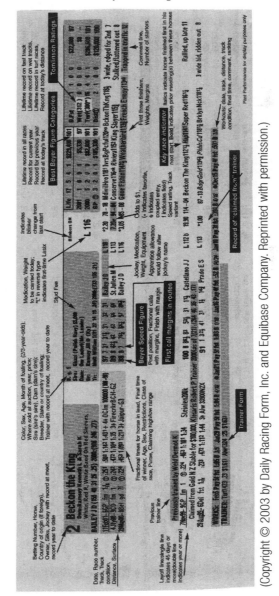

(Copyright © 2003 by Daily Racing Form, Inc. and Equibase Company. Reprinted with permission.)

APPENDIX C (cont.)

SYMBOLS & ABBREVIATIONS

3↑ Race for 3-year-olds and up

4 Race for 4-year-olds

4↑ Race for 4-year-olds and up

◆ Foreign race (outside of U.S. and Canada)

[S] Race for state-breds only

[R] Restricted race for horses who meet certain conditions

(F) Race for fillies, or fillies and mares

(T) Main turf course

[T] Inner turf course

⊗ Race originally scheduled for turf but contested on the main track, typically due to rain

[•] Inner dirt track

[D] Disqualified (symbol located next to odds and in company line, if horse is among first three finishers)

[DH] Dead Heat (symbol located in company line if horses are among first three finishers)

⚬ Dead Heat (symbol used next to finish position)

● Bullet denoting best workout of day at the distance at the track

* About distance

+ Start from turf chute

(Copyright © 2003 by Daily Racing Form, Inc. and Equibase Company. Reprinted with permission.)

APPENDIX D

Saddling Paddock Checklist

Before each race, the horses are assembled in the saddling paddock. The saddling paddock is the area in which the racing saddle and other equipment are placed on the horse. It is here that the jockeys are given their instructions and are mounted upon their respective horses by the trainers. The horses and riders are then walked around the paddock before they go to the track. The saddling paddock is the best area for the racing fan to get a close-up view of the horses in order to evaluate each horse in the race. The following checklist should be used by the racing fan to properly evaluate each horse:

1. Observe the physical condition of the horse.
   Note the coat condition (shiny or dull).
   Note the muscling.
   Note the presence of sweating.

2. Observe the behavior of the horse.
   Is it calm and manageable?
   Is it alert?
   Is it anxious?
   Are the eyes and ears focused on the surroundings?
   Is it listless or dull?

3. Observe the relationship with handlers.
   Are the groom and horse getting along?
   Is the horse uncontrollable?
   Does the groom exhibit a neat and clean appearance?

5. Observe the various types of equipment on the horse.

Note the type of bandages worn.

Note the type of blinkers worn.

Note the type of noseband worn.

Note the type of bit worn.

Note whether there are any changes in equipment from the last race.

6. Observe the horse walking with and without a rider.

Does it have a rapid, anxious walk?

Is it dragging its feet?

Does it have a slow, unhurried walk?

FURTHER READING

In order to better understand the sport of horseracing, the novice should obtain as much information as possible. The following periodicals/newspapers, textbooks, and horse-related Web sites are excellent sources to learn more about this fascinating sport and are considered by most as tools of the trade.

PERIODICALS/NEWSPAPERS

The Blood Horse: The official publication of the Thoroughbred Owners and Breeders Association. A weekly Thoroughbred magazine with a focus on racing, breeding, and sales. P. O. Box 4038, Lexington, Kentucky 40544. Phone (859) 278-2361.

The Thoroughbred Times: A weekly Thoroughbred magazine with articles concerning current events as well as news concerning racing, breeding, and sales. P. O. Box 9090, Mission Viejo, California 92690. Phone (888) 499-9090.

The Daily Racing Form: A daily Thoroughbred newspaper featuring entries, results, articles on racing and breeding, and sales reports. Subscription Department, 100 Broadway, New York, New York 10005. Phone (212) 366-7696.

TEXTBOOKS

Professional Care of the Racehorse (T. A. Landers, 1995): This book is an in-depth study of the skills required to properly care for a racehorse. Chapters deal with topics such as health, equipment, restraint, vices, safety, medications, and nutrition. 460 pages. Eclipse Press, 3101 Beaumont Centre Circle, Lexington, Kentucky, 40513. Phone (859) 278-2361.

Backyard Race Horse (Janet Del Castillo, 1992): A comprehensive off-track training and development program for owners and trainers. 282 pages. Prediction Publications, 3708 Crystal Beach Road, Winter Haven, Florida 33880. Phone (813) 299-8448.

Traits Of A Winner (Carl A. Nafzger, 1994): Written by a professional Eclipse Award–winning Thoroughbred trainer. The author describes the backside of the racetrack and provides valuable information on training and selecting Thoroughbred racehorses. 282 pages. The Russell Meerdink Co., Ltd., 1555 South Park Avenue, Neenah, Wisconsin 54946. Phone (414) 725-0955.

Owning a Racehorse Without Spending a Fortune (Harold Metzel, 2003): The author explains how to choose the right partnership and the different levels of participation in each partnership. 175 pages. Eclipse Press, 3101 Beaumont Centre Circle, Lexington, Kentucky 40513. Phone: (859) 278-2361.

HORSE-RELATED WEB SITES:

American Horse Council (www.horsecouncil.org)

American Veterinary Medical Association (www.avma.org)

HayNet (www.freerein.com/haynet/index.html)

National Thoroughbred Racing Association (www.ntra.com)

The Jockey Club Information Systems, Inc. (www.tjcis.com)

Thoroughbred Owners and Breeders Association (www.TOBA.org)

GLOSSARY

ACROSS THE BOARD: A combination pari-mutuel ticket on a horse. You collect winnings if your horse finishes first, second, or third in a race.

ALLOWANCE RACE: A race in which horses must meet certain conditions set by the racing secretary to be eligible for entry. Allowance races are a step above a claiming race.

ALSO ELIGIBLE: A horse that is officially entered in a race but is not permitted to start unless a spot is made available by another starter being scratched.

ALSO RAN: Any horse that runs out of the money, or worse than a third-place finish.

APPRENTICE: A young jockey just starting out who is given from 3 to 7 pounds weight allowance.

ASTERISK: Used in front of a horse's name on a pedigree, an asterisk (*) indicates that the horse is imported from another country. The asterisk was used up until 1977, after which the country codes were used for foreign horses. Used in front of a jockey's name in a race program, an asterisk indicates the jockey is an apprentice rider.

BACKSTRETCH: The area where the horses are stabled, which is restricted to trainers, owners, grooms, and other horseracing officials and professionals. Also the straightway part of the actual track that is opposite the grandstand.

BAT: A whip used by jockeys or exercise riders in a race or workout.

BLEEDER: A horse that bleeds from the lungs (it may appear to be bleeding from the nose) due to a stressful race or workout. A horse can, in some states, be classified as a bleeder upon endoscopic examination by a veterinarian.

BLINKERS: Cup attachments to a blinker hood that restrict the horse's vision on the sides and rear.

BLOWING: Heavy breathing when a horse is tired after a race or workout.

BLOWOUT: A short, fast final workout 1 or 2 days before a race.

BREAKING OUT: When a horse suddenly begins to sweat. This condition can be caused by high temperatures, nervousness, or stress.

BREEZE WORKOUT: Where the horse is traveling at a brisk gallop but not running all out.

BUG BOY: Slang term for an apprentice jockey.

CALL: A description of a race to an audience through a public address system.

CARD: Daily program of races.

CHALK HORSE: The betting favorite in a race.

CHUTE: Straightway extensions of either the backstretch or homestretch.

CLAIMING RACE: A race in which all horses entered may be claimed (purchased) for the amount stated.

CLOCKERS: People who record the workout times of racehorses and who may supply that information to a racing publication such as *The Daily Racing Form.*

CLUBHOUSE TURN: The first turn on a racetrack after passing the grandstand and clubhouse area.

COLT: A male horse, uncastrated, less than 5 years old.

CONDITION BOOK: A book issued by the racing secretary that lists all the conditions of future races such as weight, distance, and purse. It is usually set for a 2-week period. For a horse to be eligible for a particular race, it must meet the conditions for that race.

COUPLED: Refers to horses that are running as a single betting interest in a race.

CUSHION: The surface layer of dirt on a racetrack.

DEAD HEAT: When 2 horses finish a race at exactly the same time.

DEAD WEIGHT: Lead weights carried by a jockey who cannot meet the weight requirements of a race. These dead weights are carried in a special saddle pad in whatever quantity is necessary to meet the specified weight requirement.

DECLARE: To remove a horse from a race after it is officially entered (to scratch).

DOGS: Wooden horses or rubber traffic cones set up on the track just outside the inside rail to keep horses off the rail in morning workouts. These dogs preserve that part of the track for the afternoon races.

DRIVING: A horse traveling at full speed and all out at the end of a workout or race. Also controlling a horse from the rear, usually with a harness, some type of cart, and long driving lines attached to the bit.

ENTRY: Usually 2 or more horses entered in a race that are owned or trained by the same person. A bettor gets to bet on all the horses in an entry for the price of one.

FAST TRACK: Dry surface on which horses will usually run fast at fast times.

FATIGUE: When a horse can no longer physically maintain its speed or level of exertion. A fatigued horse should be rested in order to replenish body fluids and avoid injury.

FIELD: The horses entered into a race. Also a single betting interest of all horses over and above 12 entries.

FILLY: A female horse, under 5 years old, not used for breeding.

FORM: The past performance of a racehorse; often a table giving details relating to a horse's past performance.

FURLONG: A unit of measurement used on the racetrack to designate 1/8 mile. There are 8 furlongs in a mile.

FUTURITY: A type of race, usually a stake race, strictly for 2-year-old colts and/or fillies.

GAP: An opening on the outer wall of the racetrack to allow horses to enter and exit the stable area.

GELDING: A male horse that has been castrated (both testicles removed surgically).

HAND RIDE: When a jockey or exercise rider urges the horse to perform its best by using the hands and not the whip.

HANDICAP RACE: A race in which the horses carry weight based on their past performances; the better the horse, the more weight it will be assigned.

HANDILY: Racing or working with little effort or urging.

HOMESTRETCH: The last straight stretch of track before the finish wire, directly in front of the grandstand.

HUNG: When a horse becomes tired and slows down at the end of a race.

IMPOST: The amount of weight that is carried by a horse in a race.

INFIELD: The area of a racetrack that is situated within the inside rail.

INQUIRY: Stewards' investigation into any possible infractions of the rules during a race.

IN THE MONEY: Those horses finishing first, second, or third in a race.

LEAD PONY: A horse used to lead a racehorse to the starting gate to keep the racehorse quiet and calm. A lead pony is also used in the morning workouts to accompany a racehorse to and from the racetrack.

LENGTH: A unit of measurement of distance between horses in a race. A length is the number of feet from the nose to the tail (about 8 feet).

LUGGING IN: To suddenly bear in toward the inside rail during a race or workout.

LUGGING OUT: To suddenly bear out toward the outside rail during a race or workout.

MAIDEN: A horse that has never won a race.

MARE: A mature female horse 5 years old or over.

MORNING GLORY: A horse that trains well in morning workouts but fails to perform well in the afternoon.

MUDDER: A horse that runs unusually well on a sloppy, muddy, or heavy racetracks.

OVERNIGHT: A race for which entries close as late as the day preceding the race. Also the rough printed draft of the next day's schedule of entries.

PLACE: To finish second in a horse race.

POCKET: When a horse is surrounded by other horses during a race. This situation usually causes the horse to lose concentration.

Poles: Markers along the rail of a racetrack that designate distance, such as the 1/4-mile pole or the 1/2-mile pole. Poles are usually marked in different colors for quick identification.

Pool: Total amount of money wagered to win, place, and show as well as in exotic wagering.

Post position: The number of the stall in the starting gate from which the horse breaks in a race.

Post time: The designated time when all horses entered in a race are expected to arrive at the post, or starting gate.

Pulling up: The gradual slowing down of a horse either during or after a workout or race.

Purse: The total money that is divided among the owners of those horses officially entered in a race.

Rate: When a rider holds a horse back to save the horse's speed for the end of the race or until the rider is ready to make a bid to overtake the leaders. Often, the leaders attempt to rate their horses to save some speed for fending off challengers.

Refuser: A horse that refuses to break from the starting gate.

Receiving barn: Barn where horses coming from different racetracks are isolated just before their race.

Salute: When a jockey raises the whip to the stewards after a race, requesting permission to dismount.

Scratch: To withdraw a horse from a race in which it was formally entered.

Show: To finish third in a horse race.

Spit box: Slang term used to describe the barn where saliva, urine, and blood samples are taken by veterinarians before and after a race. Horses finishing first, second, or third as well as any other horse the veterinarians wish to spot test must go to the spit box after a race.

STAKE MONEY: Bonus money sometimes given to grooms when one of the horses in their care or when one of the other horses in the stable wins a stake race.

STAKE RACE: A race that has paid entry fees (by the racehorse owners) added to the purse. Stake races are considered the most prestigious class of races.

STATE RACING COMMISSION: The state organization that establishes and enforces rules and regulations governing racing in that state.

TAILING OFF: A horse that is gradually losing its peak form.

TONGUE TIE: A rubber band or strip of cloth or nylon used to tie the horse's tongue down to the lower jaw in order to prevent the horse from playing with its tongue during a race or workout.

TWO-MINUTE LICK: A slow exercise session in which a horse runs the distance of 1 mile in 2 minutes. The horse will run an average of 15 seconds for each 1/8 mile.

UNDER WRAPS: When a rider restrains a horse from performing at its peak during exercise.

VALET: Person assigned to care for a jockey's equipment, assist the trainer in saddling the horse, help untack the horse after a race, and carry the saddle back to the jockey's room.

WALKING RING: An oval area located near the saddling paddock where horses are walked before a race. The jockeys mount their horses in the walking ring prior to entering the racetrack.

WASHY (or **WASH OUT**): When a horse breaks out in a sweat due to heat and humidity or nervousness before a race.

Works: Training sessions that are normally scheduled early in the morning every day at a racetrack.

Weight allowance: The amount of weight given to a horse and/or rider to make them level with the competition. For example, a filly running in the Kentucky Derby only has to carry 121 pounds, whereas a colt must carry 126 pounds. In this case, the filly is given a weight allowance of 5 pounds.

Winner: The horse whose nose reaches the finish wire first.

Winner's circle: The area on the frontside where the winning horse, jockey, trainer, owner, and groom go immediately after a race for awards and/or photographs.

ACKNOWLEDGEMENTS

The author gratefully acknowledges the many people who contributed their time and effort to make the production of this book possible.

Hallie I. McEvoy, student, author, and friend for initiating the publishing process; my dear friend, Joel Silva, who provided most of the photographs appearing in this book; Maureen Sheehan for her computer expertise in formulating the final manuscript; Regan Montemayor and the Breeders' Cup, Ltd., for their contribution and review of the Breeders Cup World Thoroughbred Championship section of the book; *The Daily Racing Form* for their contribution to the text; the Mercier family of Knoll Farm and Jim Bisset of Willow Keep Farms for the use of their horses for some of the photographs in the text; Dawn Roberto for her professional typing of the final manuscript; Edward L. Kinney, president of Thoro'Bred Racing Plates, Inc., for his contribution on horseshoes; Dean A. Hoffman of the United States Trotting Association for information and photographs on Standardbreds; Gerry Mora for his expert photography; Courtney Kegley for her computer assistance; David Prine for his professional horsemanship and valuable assistance in preparing some of the photographs appearing in the book; and finally, my wife Jeriann and daughter Meghan for their moral support and patience during the writing of this book.

INDEX

ABOUT THE AUTHOR

T. A. "Ted" Landers, a licensed thoroughbred trainer, has been employed within the horse industry for the past 40 years in various capacities. He began his career by breaking thoroughbred yearlings at Claiborne Farm, Paris, Kentucky. He was a groom and exercise rider for the racing stables of Frank Whiteley Jr. and son David Whiteley, where he had the opportunity to work with such notable thoroughbreds as Sarsar, Honorable Miss, Coastal, Revidere, Forego, and the immortal Ruffian. His career with horses has also included many other occupations, such as veterinary assistant at major New York thoroughbred racetracks, livestock insurance broker, livestock insurance adjuster, equine appraiser, equine expert witness, pedigree researcher, and Jockey Club registration clerk.

Landers is an active member of many horse-related organizations, including Nassau Suffolk Horseman's Association, New York Thoroughbred Horsemen's Association, American Horsemanship Safety Association, Certified Horseman's Association, and the New York Equine Educators Association. Landers recently retired as the Director/Instructor of the New York State Vocational Equine Science Program for the Board of Cooperative Educational Services of Western Suffolk County, New York. He is presently the head instructor for the groom development program, sponsored by the New York Thoroughbred Trainers Association, at Belmont Park Racetrack.